EURO Advanced Tutorials on Operational Research

Series Editors

M. Grazia Speranza, Brescia, Italy
José Fernando Oliveira, Porto, Portugal

More information about this series at http://www.springer.com/series/13840

Michalis Doumpos • Christos Lemonakis •
Dimitrios Niklis • Constantin Zopounidis

Analytical Techniques in the Assessment of Credit Risk

An Overview of Methodologies and Applications

Springer

Michalis Doumpos
School of Production Engineering
and Management
Technical University of Crete
Chania, Greece

Dimitrios Niklis
Department of Accounting and Finance
Western Macedonia University
of Applied Sciences
Kozani, Greece

Christos Lemonakis
Department of Business Management
University of Applied Sciences Crete
Crete, Greece

Constantin Zopounidis
School of Production Engineering
and Management
Technical University of Crete
Chania, Greece

Audencia Business School
Institute of Finance
Nantes, France

ISSN 2364-687X ISSN 2364-6888 (electronic)
EURO Advanced Tutorials on Operational Research
ISBN 978-3-030-07599-6 ISBN 978-3-319-99411-6 (eBook)
https://doi.org/10.1007/978-3-319-99411-6

This Springer imprint is published by the registered company Springer Nature Switzerland AG
The registered company address is: Gewerbestrasse 11, 6330 Cham, Switzerland

Preface

Over the past few decades, the financial sector has been under continuous changes in all areas of designing, implementing, and managing the services and products provided to consumers, firms, and investors. One of the most notable changes involves the extensive use of analytical modeling techniques for financial decision making and risk management. Financial models not only provide the basis for describing financial phenomena in a normative context, but they further provide prescriptive support in designing actions to specific decision instances.

Among the many areas of financial decision making, credit risk modeling has attracted a lot of interest among academics and practitioners. The expansion of credit over the years for consumers and corporations creates a lot of challenges for measuring and managing the risks that the rising debt burden poses. Naturally, financial institutions providing credit are the ones most interested in analytical tools for credit risk management. The same also applies to the non-financial sector, given that almost all types of corporations rely on providing credit to customers and obtaining credit by creditors. The rising debt burden for households further highlights the importance of credit risk for individual consumers. Moreover, regulatory authorities and supervisors are heavily interested in assessing and monitoring the credit risk exposures for financial institutions, corporations, and the whole economy.

The measurement and management of credit risk has attracted a lot of interest over the years, not only in terms of regulatory procedures, but also as far as it concerns the use of sophisticated analytical models and new technologies. This book focuses on models and systems for credit risk scoring and rating. Such approaches are fundamental ingredients of credit risk management systems, providing estimates about the risk level and creditworthiness of consumer and corporate borrowers. The aim of the book is to provide an overview of this field, the main techniques and modeling approaches for constructing credit risk analysis systems, the validation procedures, as well as their implementation in actual instances. Moreover, the book also discusses the framework underlying the design and development of credit scoring/rating and risk assessment models. The approaches presented in this book cover both traditional financial models as well as data-driven empirical systems based on analytical methodologies from operations research, decision analysis, and artificial intelligence.

The presentation is made in a way that is accessible to readers who may not have strong financial or analytical background. Thus, the book introduces the reader to the main ideas and techniques in an accessible manner, while also covering the recent state-of-the-art advances in the literature.

The book is organized into five chapters. Chapter 1 covers the fundamentals of credit risk modeling, the status of this area, the regulatory context, as well as some key financial models for credit risk assessment. Chapter 2 provides an introduction to credit scoring and rating systems, including issues such as modeling aspects, data requirements, and the framework for developing and testing such models and systems. Chapter 3 presents an overview of different analytical modeling techniques from various fields, such as statistical models, machine learning, and multicriteria decision aid. Performance measurement issues are also discussed. Chapter 4 presents applications of analytical models to corporate and consumer credit risk assessment and illustrates comparative results and the insights that such models provide. The book closes with Chap. 5, which focuses on a discussion of some important open issues for future research in this area.

Chania, Greece
June 2018

Michalis Doumpos
Christos Lemonakis
Dimitrios Niklis
Constantin Zopounidis

Contents

Chapter 1
Introduction to Credit Risk Modeling and Assessment

1.1 Introduction

Credit is a fundamental tool for financial transactions in the private and public sector, involving both corporations and consumers. Credit provides the liquidity needed to develop all forms of economic activity, as well as funding sources for daily operations and long-term investments. While credit has a long history that dates to the early dates of civilization, over the past decades it has undergone major changes, not only in terms of its volume, but also as far as it concerns the channels through which credit is provided, the types of credit that are available, as well as the regulatory framework that defines how credit is provided.

In this new context, the risk that is associated with providing credit has become a major point of concern for all organizations that are involved with credit transactions and their supervision. In simple terms, credit risk refers to the likelihood that a borrower (obligor) will not meet future debt obligations in accordance with the terms agreed when credit was provided by a lender.

Typically, credit risk is considered in the context of financial institutions, such as banks, that provide credit to their customers in the form of corporate and consumer loans. However, credit risk is also relevant for the non-financial sector. For example, in their daily operation, firms in industry and commerce, receive credit from their suppliers and provide credit to their customers. Firms collaborating with partners of low creditworthiness may face severe financial and operating difficulties, in case their suppliers or customers face financial distress and failure.

Table 1.1 provides some illustrative data derived from the Bank of International Settlements, on the expansion of credit to the private non-financial sector (non-financial corporations and households-HHs) in the Eurozone area and USA, between the beginning of 2000 and the end of 2016. In the Eurozone, the total credit (in absolute terms, i.e., in euros) increased by 105.5%, reaching 17,481 billion euros. The increase was even higher in the USA (123.5%), where the total credit in 2016

M. Doumpos et al., *Analytical Techniques in the Assessment of Credit Risk*, EURO Advanced Tutorials on Operational Research,
https://doi.org/10.1007/978-3-319-99411-6_1

Table 1.1 Credit to the private non-financial sector in the Eurozone and USA

		Euros/US Dollars (billions)				% of GDP			
		Total	Corp.	HHs	Banks	Total	Corp.	HHs	Banks
Eurozone	2000	8505	5323	3182	5357	127.5	79.8	47.7	80.3
	2016	17,481	11,187	6294	9864	162.9	104.2	58.6	91.9
	% change	105.5	110.2	97.8	84.1	27.8	30.6	22.9	14.4
USA	2000	12,627	6027	6600	4483	130.7	62.4	68.3	46.4
	2016	28,227	13,471	14,756	9749	152	72.5	79.5	52.5
	% change	123.5	123.5	123.6	117.5	16.3	16.2	16.4	13.1

exceeded $28,200 billion (compared to $12,627 billion in 2000). When compared to gross domestic product (GDP), the relative increases appear to be more moderate: 27.8% in the Eurozone (from 127.5% of GDP in 2000 to 162.9% in 2016) and 16.3% in the USA. However, in both regions, the level of private debt to the non-financial sector is over 150% of GDP. Moreover, it is interesting to observe the composition of the debt. In the Eurozone, the credit to non-financial corporations, accounts for about 63% of the total, reaching 11,187 billion euros at the end of 2016 (104.2% of GDP), with an increase of 110.2% compared to 2000 (in absolute terms). In the USA, the total credit to households exceeds that involving non-financial corporations. At the end of 2016, the total credit to US households reached $14,756 billion (approximately 52% of the total), with an increase of over 123% since 2000 (in absolute terms). Finally, it is worth noting the contribution of the banking sector. In the Eurozone, the total private credit provided by banks in 2016 was 9864 billion euros with an increase of 84.1% compared to 2000. In comparison to the total credit, the contribution of banks decreased to 56.4% from 63% in 2000. In the USA, the contribution of the banking sector is lower (around 35% of the total), with the credit provided by banks reaching $9749 billion in 2016.

The above statistics highlight the rapid credit expansion over the past two decades, as well as the role of credit for the non-financial sector, including corporations and consumers. In addition to these statistics, it is also worth noting the widespread use of new complex financial instruments, many of which entail credit risk, such as credit derivatives (e.g., credit default swaps, collateralized debt obligations). Credit derivatives are bilateral contracts used to manage credit risk exposure, usually traded over the counter (i.e., they are customized between the two parties involved and they are not supervised through established exchanges). Moreover, over the past decade new financing systems and platforms have emerged, based on technologies such as social lending, peer-to-peer lending, and crowdfunding, raising new challenges for monitoring the expansion of credit and assessing the risks involved.

In this context, the management of credit risk has become a multifaceted issue with different regulatory/supervisory, methodological, and technical challenges. Similarly to other areas in risk management, credit risk management is a complex process, which is involved with the analysis, assessment, and monitoring of credit risk in financial transactions. Credit risk management has changed dramatically over the past couple of decades, and it still evolves at all levels. These changes are mostly evident in financial institutions (e.g., banks) and providers of credit risk management solutions, but implicitly they affect all organizations exposed to credit risk.

A first major development that has transformed the area of credit risk managements, involves the regulatory framework, mainly as far as credit institutions (e.g., banks) are concerned. In 1988, the Basel Committee on Banking Supervision, introduced the first set of rules regarding the capital requirements that banks should meet. This set of rules, known as the Basel I Accord (or simply Basel I), imposed simplistic guidelines for credit risk management based on a weighting scheme of a bank's assets, depending on their level of risk. In 2004, the Basel II Accord introduced a much more refined framework, covering not only credit risk, but also operational and market risks. Moreover, it added guidelines and rules regarding supervisors as well as reporting and market discipline. The third accord (Basel III) is currently under development and it is expected to be implemented until 2019, bringing more strict capital requirements together with provisions about liquidity and bank leverage (i.e., the use of equity capital versus total risk exposure). A key point of this brief historical overview is that credit risk is a highly regulated topic in financial services, with a very broad set of rules and requirements imposed on the design, implementation, and monitoring of credit risk management practices.

The second major development involves the widespread use of analytical methods for credit risk modeling and management. Early credit risk management was primarily based on empirical evaluation systems. CAMEL has been the most widely used system in this context, which is based on the empirical combination of several factors related to Capital, Assets, Management, Earnings, and Liquidity. It was soon realized however, that such empirical systems cannot provide a solid and objective basis for credit risk management. This led to a growing need for the development of more advanced approaches. The roots of such approaches can be traced back to the 1960–1970s with the development of the first bankruptcy prediction models and the late 1980s with the introduction of the first credit scoring model by Fair Isaac Co., in the USA (FICO score). The use of analytical models, intensified with the tightening regulatory framework described above, which promoted the use of analytical systems by providing incentives to credit institutions to implement such approaches. These incentives involved relaxed capital requirements for institutions that used sophisticated analytical models, as opposed to the implementation of simpler empirical alternatives. This trend towards analytical credit risk modeling, was further facilitated by the rapid advances in a wide range of analytical disciplines, including mathematical finance, data science, as well as operations research.

Analytical credit risk modeling applies both to individual loans as well as credit portfolios. In the former case, the objective is to assess the creditworthiness of an obligor and the expected loss from granting credit. At this stage credit scoring and rating models and systems are used. The principles and details of such models/systems are discussed in Chaps. 2 and 3. The outputs of the analysis at the loan level constitute the fundamental basis for credit portfolio management. At this higher level, the analysis extends to a collection (portfolio) of loans that an organization has. The portfolio analysis provides loss estimates for all loans, thus guiding decisions for setting targets for capital requirements, portfolio diversification, and facilitates the preparation of reports for internal/external audit and control.

Of course, with the outbreak of the global credit crisis in 2007–2008, credit risk models (and other financial models, too) received a lot of criticism about their role in promoting the credit expansion prior to the crisis and their failure to provide reliable estimates of the true risk exposure. On the one hand, it is true that the widespread adoption and use of credit risk models has facilitated the expansion of credit, by lowering risk premiums for corporate clients and consumers. Thus, access to credit financing became cheaper. Moreover, despite the advances made in the theory and practice of credit risk measurement, there have been some noticeable misses, that have naturally casted doubts and raised criticism. On the other hand, it should be pointed out, that credit risk models are not crystal balls and limitations do exist. Similarly to all financial models, credit risk models involve complex socio-economic phenomena, which are, by definition, impossible to describe in full accuracy. Despite that, analytical decision making, strategic planning, supervisory control, the design of new financing products and services would all be impossible without credit risk models.

1.2 Credit Risk Management for Financial Institutions

Traditionally, financial institutions managed credit portfolios by business lines. This approach led to divergent practices regarding risk ratings, parameter estimation, limits, and a variety of other portfolio metrics. As a result, it was difficult to aggregate credit risk or even to compare businesses. The arrival of economic capital models and the requirements of Basel II changed this approach. Just as the management of market risk has been centralized, one can make a strong case for having a central view of credit risk throughout the organization. Such a view ensures a standard and consistent approach to measurement, monitoring, and control. It is important to note that a business line perspective and a central view of credit portfolio management are not mutually exclusive. Many organizations will adopt a structure that recognizes the need to balance both business-unit issues and firm-wide perspectives. Under such an approach, the portfolio management discipline can ensure consistent integration of enterprise-wide strategic objectives such as risk appetite across the organization, while individual business units can also be sure their tactical issues are addressed. In practice, it is difficult to manage all credit risks across an organization. For this reason, organizations typically begin their portfolio management effort by first addressing their bulkiest exposures, which tend to be the large exposures to corporate borrowers. Once practices and principles around managing these exposures are in place, resources can then be directed toward tackling the remaining pockets of credit risk in the organization.

Banking institutions traditionally manage credit portfolios per business activity. This approach leads to various practices in relation to credit risk assessments, parameter estimation by loan portfolio category, risk taking and other characteristics that make up a bank's loan portfolio.

In a context of consistent risk assessment, it is difficult to assess the underlying credit risk or even to compare companies that have bank loans and are included in the credit portfolio of a credit institution. The adoption of economic capital models and the regulatory requirements set out in Basel II and Basel III have strengthened the framework for joint assessment and management of loan portfolios.

Under such an approach, a loan portfolio discipline can incorporate a bank's strategic goals, such as risk margins, the handling of large borrowers or borrowers with high default rates (i.e., mainly borrowers with overdue debt to the credit institution over 90 days), which tend to be large exposures to corporate borrowers. As long as consistent loan management practices are applied, better and more representative management of their available resources is provided.

1.3 Uncertainties and Risk Factors

It is not disputed today that credit is a central feature of economic activity. Without it, the financial units would not be able to spend money that they do not have, using their future income, to meet their current needs. Borrowing, however, in any form, involves the notion of uncertainty. Credit institutions know in advance that some of their clients will either have difficulty or will not be able to repay their loan obligations. For this reason, they need to address this uncertainty and have appropriate tools and techniques to predict the future course of credit for each potential customer.

Uncertainty in providing credit takes the following three main forms:

- **Strategic uncertainty**, referring to ignorance of the real intentions and character of the debtor. Uncertainty has two strategic elements that economic theory often fails to handle in an appropriate way: unfavorable choice and moral credit risk. Creditors face the problem of unfavorable choice because if credit risk is valued in terms of interest rate in relation to the risk assumed, a consistent borrower must be treated more favorably compared to a less consistent one. Given a group of borrowers in a certain credit category and a fixed interest rate, those who are consistent and have good credit characteristics are charged interest rates higher than the actual risk borne by the creditor, compared with the lesser or even more and inconsistent debtors, who will pay a lower real interest rate than they should, based on their credit ratings. Taking credit is therefore more profitable for those who are less likely to repay it, with bad borrowers moving away from the market, thus creating a vicious circle where more bad borrowers lead to higher interest rates, which discourage good borrowers from using credit. The unfavorable choice is reinforced in credit card purchases, where credit is granted to individuals for general use, rather than for specific transactions or even for a predetermined period.

The second strategic element is moral hazard. Borrowing in unfavorable terms increases a borrower's risk and tends to increase the probability of default. In other words, a higher interest rate pushes the borrower towards insolvency. This may lead eventually to changes in the borrower's lending position by increasing his/her alternative sources of credit. For example, moral hazard is exacerbated with credit cards lending by the fact that people are likely to resort to credit cards debt to get credit in times of their financial difficulty, giving it the role of the of the last resort lender.

- **Occasional uncertainty**, resulting from the lack of knowledge of exogenous factors that cannot be controlled by the borrower. Many people become economically insolvent due to situations that they cannot predict and make them unable to repay their debts. Loss of work, the emergence of an extraordinary economic need, a severe economic crisis at the regional or country level, the irregular and drastic political changes that are common mainly in emerging markets, can significantly affect the ability of a borrower to meet existing debt obligations. Unexpected major natural disasters can also lead to economic havoc, even for economically sound borrowers.
- **Cognitive uncertainty**, resulting from a borrower's misconception of his/her actual status regarding the use of credit and the coverage of existing and new loan payments. For instance, consumers often adopt irrational financial behavior, making expenses that exceed their real economic capacity. They are willing to be charged with high interest rates, transferring their debts within the time limits or near the end of their billing period. Whenever uncertainty cannot be measured satisfactorily, the economic actors involved in the provision of credit should rely on the trust of their clients to support their co-operation and financial transactions. This expectation includes, among other things, competence, accountability and mutual interest. Moreover, the notion of trust is contrasted with the established risk assessment of credit. Trust is not a factor that can be easily quantified. Instead, it determines important qualitative characteristics of the borrower-debtor relationship.

Having in mind these types of uncertainties, one can identify several factors that create risk in decision making regarding credit granting. Among others, the following factors can be described:

- Depreciations in the value of guarantees (i.e., short-term financing provided on an existence of a contractual base with the use of decreasing in values guarantees, such as collaterals, securities, etc.).
- Over-indebtedness of the borrower to the extent that it is no longer possible existing obligations to be repaid.
- Inadequate supervision of the solvency, liquidity, and the qualitative characteristics of the borrower that affect his/her ability to repay the loan.
- The non-systematic application of approved guidelines for collaterals and guarantees depending on the risk exposure (exposure at default).

- Differences on approval specifications for low-value loans between different branches of the financial institution, because of localities or other special authorization techniques enforced.
- Poor management practices and budgetary control.
- The use of some or all the loans for different purposes for which they were approved.
- Duration of the loan, as short-term allocations are generally less risky compared to long-term liabilities, due to the increasing uncertainty over longer time horizons.
- Legal issues, omissions, misunderstandings and errors.
- Lack of insurance coverage against unexpected events that could affect the borrower's economic status and his/her ability to repay the loan.

1.4 Elements of Credit Risk Modeling

The main outcome of credit risk modeling and management systems is an estimate of the expected loss for a loan over a specific period, which is usually set to be one year, in accordance with the standard time basis used for financial reporting. The expected loss (*EL*) has three main components and can be expressed as follows:

$$EL = PD \times EAD \times LGD$$

The three main components involved in this estimation, are the following:

1. Probability of default (PD): PD represents the likelihood that the obligor will not meet scheduled loan payments during the period of the analysis (i.e., the likelihood of default). The standard definition of default is when there is a payment delay by at least 90 days, but more refined options for defining default events may also be used (e.g., considering also the amount due). PD is usually estimated with analytical models, known as credit scoring/rating models, considering several factors about the status of the obligor. The structure and development of such models will be discussed in detail in Chaps. 2 and 3.
2. Exposure at default (EAD): EAD is the risk exposure at the time of default (i.e., the amount of capital that is due to be repaid). EAD mostly depends on the characteristics of the loan, rather than the obligor. For some types of loans (e.g., a simple loan or a bond), EAD is easy to specify, because the time when payments are made, and the amounts involved are fixed. In other cases, however, the estimation of EAD may be more involved. A simple example is credit cards for which the outstanding amount varies over time.
3. Loss given default (LGD): The final component of expected loss, is the loss in the case default occurs. LGD is expressed as a percentage of EAD. Usually, LGD

ranges between 0 and 100% and it is often defined through the complementary concept of recovery rate (recovery rate = 100 % −LGD). LGD depends on several factors that define the type of default and how it is resolved, including the characteristics of the obligor and the loan, as well as the macroeconomic environment. For instance, LGD for corporate loans may be affected by the size of the firm, its business sector, and its financial status. Loan-specific characteristics include factors related to collateral and loan seniority, among others. In the simplest setting, LGD may be defined based purely on historical data regarding specific types of loans, but with the introduction of the Basel II Accord, more sophisticated approaches, based on statistical LGD estimation models, are usually preferred.

The estimation of the expected loss for a loan is the basic element for portfolio risk analysis. The rest of the discussion in this book will concentrate on models for estimating the probability of default, which is the most fundamental element of credit risk analysis.

1.5 The Regulatory Framework for Financial Institutions

Financial institutions are subject to tight supervision by regulatory authorities regarding the processes followed for measuring, managing, and reporting credit risk exposures. The attempt to formalize of set of standard international guidelines started with the first Basel Accord in 1988, which was revised through Basel II that is currently active. Under the existing requirements all financial institutions should have enough capital to meet the risk of their assets. This is expressed in the form of capital adequacy ratios (CAR) of the form:

$$\text{CAR} = \frac{\text{Capital}}{\text{Risk} - \text{weighted assets}} \geq \alpha$$

where α is the minimum requirement imposed by the regulator (e.g., $\alpha = 8\%$, under the Basel II setting), capital refers to tier 1 and tier 2 capital,[1] and risk-weighted assets (RWA) is a weighted average of the assets that a financial institution has, with weights defined based on their risk.

Under the Basel II guidelines, financial institutions have two options for calculating their RWA based on different implementations of the risk modeling framework outlined in the previous section. Under the basic scheme, which is referred to as the standardized approach, prescribed risk estimates (risk weights) are used. These prescribed inputs are set by a supervisory authority and are common to all cases without taking into consideration any sophisticated risk assessment approach

[1]Tier 1 is the core capital (i.e., equity and reserves) which is the primary source of funds that a financial institution may use to cover unexpected losses. Tier 2 capital refers to supplementary sources of funds, which are not as secure as tier 1 capital.

customized to the characteristics of specific loans, portfolios, or financial institution. Moreover, risk assessment is based on external models. Naturally, adopting such an approach is costlier for financial institutions, because capital requirements are higher to account for the ambiguity of the standardized approach.

Alternatively, a financial institution can employ the internal ratings-based approach (IRB) which provides more flexibility but requires the adoption of sophisticated modeling systems based on historical data. Under this scheme, internal credit rating/scoring systems can be used to assess the probability of default, using historical databases within a financial institution. LGD assessments can also be done through internal statistical models (advanced IRB) or be set according to prescribed norms defined by supervisors (foundation IRB). In the IRB approach, regulatory capital requirements for unexpected losses are derived from risk weight functions, which are based on the so-called Asymptotic Risk Factor (ASFR) model. The ASFR model framework assumes that a bank's credit portfolio is completely diversified, which implies that idiosyncratic risks associated with individual exposures tend to cancel out one-another and only systematic risk has a material effect on portfolio losses. This allows financial institutions to calculate capital charges on a loan-by-loan basis and then aggregate these up at the portfolio level. For instance, for a corporate exposure, RWA is defined as

$$RWA = K \times 12.5 \times EAD$$

where K denotes the capital requirement, which is a function of PD, LGD, the maturity of the loan (M) and an asset correction parameter (R):

$$K = \left[LGD \times N\left(\frac{N^{-1}(PD)}{\sqrt{1-R}} + N^{-1}(0.999)\sqrt{\frac{R}{1-R}} \right) - PD \times LGD \right] \frac{1+(M-2.5)\beta}{1-1.5\beta}$$

where N is the cumulative standard normal distribution function and N^{-1} is its inverse, R the asset correlation parameter and β a maturity adjustment:

$$\beta = [0.11852 - 0.05478\log(PD)]^2$$

The asset correlation term is used to take into consideration the borrower's dependence on the general state of the economy, and it is computed by a specific formula defined by the Basel Committee. The formula incorporates two empirical observations. Firstly, asset correlations decrease with increasing PD, which means that the higher the probability of default, the higher the idiosyncratic risk components of an obligor. Secondly, asset correlations increase with firm size, which means that larger firms are more closely related to the general conditions in the economy, while smaller firms are more likely to default due to idiosyncratic reasons.

Maturity effects are incorporated in the above model as a function of both maturity and the probability of default. The function's form is based on the following considerations. Firstly, long-term borrowers are riskier than the short-term borrowers; downgrades are more likely to happen for long-term borrowers. Consequently, the capital requirement should increase with maturity. Secondly, low PD borrowers have more potential to downgrade than high PD borrowers. Thus, maturity adjustments should be higher for low PD borrowers.

As mentioned above, the asymptotic capital formula has been derived under the assumption that a bank's credit portfolio is perfectly diversified. In real-world portfolios though, there is always a residual of undiversified idiosyncratic risk components. If this residual risk is ignored, then the true capital requirements will be underestimated. Therefore, the Basel Committee proposes the calculation, on a portfolio level, of the so-called granularity adjustments. Granularity is a measurement of the portfolio's concentration risk; the additional risk resulting from increased exposure to one-obligor or groups of correlated obligors. These adjustments can be either negative or positive, depending on the portfolio's diversification level.

The framework of Basel II is refined in various aspects in the upcoming Basel III Accord, which is expected to be fully implemented in 2019. Basel III introduces several changes to strengthen risk measurement in a particularly volatile economic environment. For instance, under the new framework higher capital adequacy standards are imposed (CAR $\geq$10.5%). Leverage and liquidity requirements are also imposed. Moreover, Basel III puts emphasis on counterparty credit risk, which involves the credit risk in derivatives transactions and securitization products. Finally, except for tighter capital requirements, Basel III introduces a new framework to achieve better governance and more effective risk management. An extended procedure including stress tests, model validation, and a series of test checks are established to ensure more effective risk management. The new regulatory framework introduces the testing program under extreme conditions to ensure that various risk measures fully reflect reality. In addition, stress tests are required to investigate the possibility if extreme market conditions and high volatility affect not only the exposure of banking institutions but also their credit rating.

1.6 Types of Credit Risk Assessment Approaches

There are different approaches available for assessing the likelihood of default in credit risk modeling. Their main differences involve the data required to implement them as well as their scope and range of application. Below we describe the main features of each approach, covering three main schemes based on judgmental approaches, empirical models, and financial models.

1.6.1 Judgmental Approaches

Judgmental approaches for credit risk assessment are the oldest and the simplest ones (in terms of their level of analytical sophistication). They are also referred to as qualitative approaches or expert systems, because they are based solely on the expert judgment of credit analysts of the fundamental qualitative and quantitative characteristics of the borrower.

A well-known judgmental evaluation scheme is known as "5C analysis", according to which the assessment covers five main dimensions of a borrower's creditworthiness:

1. character: the personality of the borrower,
2. capacity: the ability of the borrower to repay the loan, based on the existing income, expenses, and other debt obligations,
3. capital: the own capital of the borrower that is at risk,
4. collateral: the guarantees provided about the payment of the obligation
5. conditions: general conditions that describe the status of the business environment and the characteristics of the loan (e.g., the interest rate).

These dimensions are typically analyzed considering a broad range of qualitative and quantitative factors. For instance, for a corporate loan these may include data derived from publicly available financial statements (balance sheet, income statement, cash flow statement), information included in a business plan that is often submitted with the loan application, data about the business sector of the firm, the region it operates, the market, the general economic outlook, etc. In the case of small loans, this information is processed and analyzed by a single credit analyst or a small group of analysts, whereas for larger loans a more in-depth examination is required both by expert analysts as well as by credit committees.

Even though judgmental systems usually follow a quite detailed, structured, and systematic framework, they are based purely on expertise rather than theory or empirical data. This raises some significant limitations. For instance, it is very difficult to: (a) assess the quality of the obtained results (validation), (b) update the structure of the evaluation process and the actual results to changes in the decision environment and the available information, and (c) examine scenarios that may affect the creditworthiness of a single borrower or the risk of a whole credit portfolio. Moreover, transparency and consistency issues may arise, particularly in cases where there is a lack of clear implementation and monitoring protocols.

During the 1980s and early 1990s some attempts have been made to incorporate some analytical abilities into purely judgmental systems. These attempts mostly focused on the expert systems (ESs) technology, which was emerging during that period. ESs provided structured reasoning capabilities, often combines with database management, and can be considered as the first attempt towards more sophisticated artificial intelligence approaches that have attracted considerable interest recently.

Despite their limitations, judgmental approaches are still being used in areas where there is a lack of historical data for constructing more advanced models. A typical example is project finance, which is involved with large-scale and long-term infrastructure projects in the public and private sector. Each such project usually has unique characteristics that make it difficult to use information from past projects. Moreover, the scale of these projects requires special financing solutions, whose design and credit risk analysis need very careful consideration by different groups of experts. Other examples may include the financing in special business sectors (e.g., shipping), as well as the financing of startups and small and medium-sized enterprises (SMEs). Except for their usefulness in handling special cases, judgmental approaches may further provide deep insights into complex cases as experienced credit analysts are able to interpret correctly unstructured information from various sources in a manner that makes sense from a business and financial perspective.

1.6.2 Data-Driven Empirical Models

Data-driven approaches are based of models constructed based on historical data about loans accepted, rejected, paid as agreed, and cases in default. Such approaches are applicable to both corporate and consumer loans, when historical data are available. The relevant data can be derived from various sources, including databases maintained internally by banks and other credit institutions, as well as credit rating agencies and data providers. The data mainly involve the characteristics of the borrower and the status of the loan (i.e., distinguishing between loans in default and non-defaulted cases), together with other risk factors about the external environment. Thus, the main input information is the same as the one described earlier for judgmental models. However, instead of aggregating the available risk factors using approaches based on expertise, empirical models are constructed to identify non-trivial patterns from the data, thus leading to the formulation of explicit relationships between the likelihood of default and the input variables/risk factors. This is achieved through analytical approaches for fitting prediction models to data.

The roots of empirical approaches can be traced back to the late 1960s when the first statistical models for predicting bankruptcy were developed in the academic literature. Since then, this area has evolved rapidly driven by methodological advances on data analytics as well as advances on the preparation and collection of comprehensive data of various forms.

On the one hand, a wide variety of statistical, machine learning, and operations research techniques are now available for data analytics (data preprocessing and model construction). These allow to identify complex non-linear empirical credit default relationships in a computationally efficient manner, even for large-scale datasets. On the other hand, the extensive academic research, the enrichment of the regulatory framework, and the advances in the practice of credit risk management, have led to the identification of new relevant risk factors, which have proven useful in various contexts, beyond the traditional financial data (e.g., financial ratios), which have been widely used in the past. For instance, in corporate credit risk analysis corporate governance issues have recently emerged as important factors (e.g., issues related to business ethics, governance structure, internal audit systems, etc.). Information derived from social networks and other public information analyzed with new technologies (e.g., news analytics) are also valuable. Finally, real-time information from the financial markets (e.g., for listed companies) further enhances the structure and explanatory/predictive power of empirical models.

Except for their analytical power and the ability to analyze massive amounts of data, empirical models have several other advantages. First, they add transparency and consistency in credit risk modeling and decision making. This involves not only the outputs they provide, but also their construction and maintenance. An important issue in that direction involves the ability to validate empirical models, covering not only their underlying structure, but also their predictive power, which can be easily tested and measured against actual data. Moreover, they allow the analytical examination of hypotheses, and conducting of scenario analyses and stress testing scenarios. Finally, they can be updated in a timely manner to consider new information as soon as it becomes available and they can be customized to fit the requirements of cases, adding flexibility in the risk modeling process. For instance, special models can be developed for large companies or SMEs, for specific business sectors, as well as for various types of consumer loans such as credit cards, mortgage loans, etc.

Nevertheless, limitations and weaknesses exist too. The most important involves the reliance on historical data for predictive modeling. Due to the intrinsic nature of the financial and business world, which is characterized by deep uncertainties and high volatility, past data may not be able to fully describe future risks. This is particularly true in times of crises and financial crashes, whose scale and effects are very difficult to predict. Thus, the data used for building empirical credit risk models, are incomplete and have imperfections. Moreover, data used in empirical models are often considered as backward looking and static. For instance, the financial statements of a firm or the income of an individual is static information, only reflecting the current status of the borrower. Using expert judgement for model building and implementation, together with careful data processing, can help ameliorate some of these issues, but they cannot be completely addressed. Finally, it is worth noting that the information considered in empirical models is not updated on a real-time basis. Even though the updated data come in on a regular basis (e.g., quarterly financial statements), they may fail to incorporate the most recent facts about the status of the borrower.

Given the widespread use of such models in credit risk modeling and analysis, we will devote Chaps. 2 and 3 to present in detail the characteristics of empirical models for credit scoring and rating, covering both the model building process as well as the methodological tools that are used in this area. Applications of such models will be presented in Chap. 4.

1.6.3 Financial Models

In contrast to empirical approaches, which are data-driven, financial models are mostly based on theory. Thus, instead of the descriptive and predictive nature of data-driven models, financial models adopt a normative approach, which is founded on basic economic and financial principles that underlie the financial world. In the context of credit risk, financial models describe the mechanism of the default process. Financial models are also commonly referred to as market models, because they rely on data from financial markets. Thus, they are focused on corporate debt. Two main types of financial models for credit risk modeling can be identified, namely structural models and reduced form models. The former type of models assumes that default is an endogenous process that is linked to a firm's structural characteristics, such as the value of its assets and debt. Reduced form models adopt a different approach assuming the default is a random event that may happen at any time driven by shift in an exogenous random variable (usually a Poisson jump process). Such models use market data on bonds and credit derivatives as the main source of information about a firm's credit risk structure. In the following subsections, we describe some well-known examples of such financial models.

1.6.3.1 A Structural Model Based on Option Pricing Theory

Options are financial derivatives, in which two counterparties (the buyer and the writer/seller) agree about a future transaction on an underlying asset (e.g., equity, bonds, foreign exchange, interest rates, commodities, etc.). The buyer pays the value of the option contract to the writer and gets the right to buy or sell (depending on the type of the contract) the agreed asset from/to the writer. The writer, on the other hand, cannot opt out of the agreed transaction, should the buyer decide to exercise the option.

The capital structure of a firm can also be considered as a call option between the shareholders and the creditors, on the assets of the firm. The shareholders are the buyers of the option and the creditors are the writers. Creditors temporarily "own" a part of the company (by providing credit) and shareholders have the option to pay back the loan, if it is economically meaningful for the firm to continue its operation.

Formally, let us assume a firm with a simple debt structure, consisting of a single liability with face value L maturing at time T. From an economic perspective, it makes sense for the shareholders to pay back the debt, only if the market value of the firm (A_T) exceeds its debt; otherwise the firm's net worth is negative. Thus, at time T, the net worth of the firm (the value of option for the shareholders) is:

$$\max\{A_T - L, 0\}$$

This is exactly the terminal payoff of a call option with exercise price L on an asset with price A_T at the time the option expires. The current value of the option on the assets of the firm, is the market value of equity (E), and it is given by the well-known Black-Scholes option pricing formula:

$$E = A\mathcal{N}(d_1) - Le^{-rT}\mathcal{N}(d_2) \tag{1.1}$$

where A is current market value of the firm's assets, r is the risk-free interest rate, and $\mathcal{N}(\cdot)$ is the cumulative distribution function of the standard normal distribution defined at points:

$$d_1 = \frac{\ln\left(\frac{A}{L}\right) + \left(r + \frac{\sigma_A^2}{2}\right)T}{\sigma_A\sqrt{T}} \quad \text{and} \quad d_2 = d_1 - \sigma\sqrt{T}$$

with σ_A denoting the volatility of the assets' returns.

Furthermore, under the assumption that equity is a function of assets and time, the volatility of equity (σ_E) is given by:

$$\sigma_E = \frac{\sigma_A A \mathcal{N}(d_1)}{E} \tag{1.2}$$

Equations (1.1) and (1.2) have two unknowns, namely the current value of assets (A) and the assets' volatility (σ). All other parameters are known, including:

- the market value of equity (E): the market capitalization of the firm,
- the volatility of equity (σ_E): the annualized volatility of the firm's equity estimated from historical market data,
- the time (in years) up to the repayment of the loan (T),
- the face value of debt (L): usually taken as the short-term debt of the firm as reported in its balance sheet,
- the risk-free interest rate (r): the yield of treasury-bills or other similar low-risk securities.

The solution of the system of equations (1.1) and (1.2) for A and σ_A can be with a simple iterative Newton-type algorithm, yielding estimates about the current value of assets and the corresponding volatility. Moreover, $\mathcal{N}(-d_2)$ is the risk-neutral probability of default (probability that the shareholders will decide not to exercise the option to repay the firm's debt), derived by assuming that assets grow by the risk-free rate. To derive the real probability of failure, the expected return on assets (μ) should be used instead of the risk-free rate r. Thus, the probability of default (PD) can be expressed as follows:

$$PD = \mathcal{N}\left[-\frac{\ln\left(\frac{A}{L}\right) + \left(\mu - \frac{\sigma_A^2}{2}\right)T}{\sigma_A\sqrt{T}}\right] \tag{1.3}$$

In order to derive this PD estimate, the return on asset is required. A standard approach is to first solve (1.1) and (1.2) using historical market data and then define μ as the rate of change in A over past time periods.

Moreover, the PD estimation through Eq. (1.3) provides a measure of the distance to default (DD), defined as the number of standard deviations the firm's assets are away from the default point L:

$$DD = \frac{\ln\left(\frac{A}{L}\right) + \left(\mu - \frac{\sigma_A^2}{2}\right)T}{\sigma_A\sqrt{T}}$$

A well-known implementation of this approach is the Moody's-KMV Expected Default Frequency (EDF™) model. The main difference in Moody's-KMV approach involve the way the DD is mapped to a probability of default scale. Rather than resorting to the normal distribution as in Eq. (1.3), the EDF™ model uses historical data to derive an empirical distribution of default frequencies. Moreover, the default point is defined as the sum of short-term debt and half of long-term debt, which better approximates the actual loan obligations of a firm.

1.6.3.2 The Credit Metrics Model

The Credit Metrics method calculates the probability of default for a company by comparing it with similar companies that have defaulted on their debt. The methodology is based on a transition table that measures whether the probability of default may change over the subsequent period. Credit Metrics is therefore a mark-to-market model rather than a default mode model. Since some variables that would help in the risk analysis cannot be measured, the transition probabilities are used instead to calculate the probability of default.

The input main data used in this approach include:

- The credit rating of the issuer of the bond.
- The transition matrix of credit ratings, which shows the ability to transition one issuer from one credit rating to another (rating transition matrix).
- Recovery rates on defaulted loans (recovery rates).
- The yield margins on bond markets.

More specifically, the model should initially have all the credit ratings that the credit institution will use and the chances of transition from one category to another over a given period. The credit grades are assumed to be homogeneous. This assumption has created criticism for this model. Furthermore, the determination of the time horizon is important. This is usually set at one year, but much longer time horizons can also be considered (e.g., up to 10 years). Recovery rates are then calculated using future returns of initial funds at fixed rates. The use of fixed interest rates has also raised some concerns about the validity of the model, because interest rates for long time periods can be quite volatile. The output of the model is a distribution of the change in a loan's value over time.

More specifically, the value of a loan issue (e.g., a bond issue) given its maturity, the interest rate and the next year's rating can be defined as:

$$PV_{it} = \frac{CF_{it}}{(1 + r_t + s_{it})^t}$$

where

- PV_{it} is the value of a bond in credit grade i (i.e., the credit rating during the next period),
- CF_{it} the coupon payment at time t,
- r_t the risk-free interest rate in period t,
- s_{it} the annual risk premium for a loan in credit grade i at time t.

The above relationship can be used to derive estimates for the market value for each non-marketable loan or bond and assess the risk for both individual loans and a portfolio of loans. Using Credit Metrics, each loan may have a different risk and therefore a different capital requirement.

The Credit Metrics model provides an analytical methodology for risk quantification across a wide range of financial products, including, but not limited to, traditional loans, commitments, letters of credit, fixed income securities, commercial contracts (e.g., trade credit and claims) and products driven by the market, such as exchanges, forward contracts and other derivatives. Such an approach enables the systematic understanding of the risks and promotes transparency in credit risk management and external regulatory supervision. However, it should be noted that Credit Metrics is not a rating tool, nor a risk pricing model. Instead it is designed to provide portfolio risk measures that take account of the relationship between the assets separately and the existing portfolio, making credit risk management more systematic.

The Credit Metrics methodology evaluates credit risk at both the individual and portfolio levels in three stages. In the first, the profile of the exposure is determined. In the second, we estimate the volatility of the value of each financial product caused by revaluations, devaluations and defaults. Finally, in the third stage, considering the correlations between the above events, the volatility of individual financial products is added together to calculate the total volatility of the portfolio. This methodology is best understood by the following steps:

1. **Reporting profiles:** Credit Metrics integrates reports from conventional financial instruments, such as floating-rate bonds or unpaid loans. It also provides a framework within which less clear exposure profiles can be estimated, such as disbursed or non-interest-bearing securities, including debt obligations, letters of credit and commercial credit agreements. Credit Metrics also incorporates reports from market-based tools such as swaps and fixed rate bonds, all reporting on an equivalent basis to other financial instruments.
2. **Volatility from upgrades, downgrades, or defaults:** this step refers to estimation of the probability that a borrower will move to a higher or lower credit rating. Each result of the transition is an estimated change in value and any value result is

weighted by its risk factor to generate a breakdown of the value in each credit condition. Therefore, the estimated value of the asset can be calculated as the expected value of each asset and the standard deviation of the value.
3. **Correlations:** All individual value distributions are combined to produce a result for the entire portfolio. To measure the volatility of the portfolio's value from asset price volatility, correlation estimates are required for credit quality changes. Since correlations for credit quality cannot be easily observed by historical data, many different approaches to assessing correlations can be used, such as a simple fixed correlation, coupled with the Credit Metrics model.

1.6.3.3 The Credit Risk$^+$ Model

The Credit Risk$^+$ model was developed by Credit Suisse Financial Products in 1997. In contrast to the KMV model, it does not use the capital structure of the company as it is not related to its credit rating and hence to the probability of default.

The Credit Metrics model attempts to assess the debt securities and the losses they may incur to the financial institution. On the other hand, the Credit Risk$^+$ model only distinguishes two credit events, a bankruptcy situation and a bad credit condition. Moreover, according to this model, a credit institution's losses are possible only in the event of bankruptcy and perceives the default frequency as a continuous random variable.

In this model, for a portfolio it is considered that the probability of a borrower defaulting on his obligations is very small and independent of the remaining credit events. The distribution that best suits this model is the Poisson distribution, which suggests that the average default rate should be equal to its variance. Finally, in contrast to Credit Metrics, the Credit Risk$^+$ model does not calculate credit ratings but only default events. The advantage of this model, since it focuses mainly on the fact of default, is the minimum data required and is therefore particularly easy to use.

1.7 Measuring the Financial Performance of Loans

Although many credit risk assessment methodologies based on scoring and rating models, as those analyzed in Chaps. 2 and 3, are often validated through statistical performance measures, the outcomes they provide in terms of daily decision making are assessed and reported in financial terms. Therefore, it is important to understand the financial measures that are used to assess the performance of a loan and make acceptance/rejection decisions based on the return of the loan in relation to its risk. Such financial decision criteria complement analytical credit risk models, taking into consideration additional decision factors, regarding regulatory requirements, fees, the cost of capital, etc.

The most commonly used financial performance measure is risk-adjusted return on capital (RAROC). RAROC has become one of the main concerns of the financial industry and the reason is that efficient risk management of a portfolio is a key factor for the profitability of financial institutions. Indeed, what distinguishes the modern economies than those of the past is the new ability to locate risk, measuring it, assessing its consequences, and then taking it such as mitigation.

RAROC is a performance measure used to assess the performance of a financial institution (i.e., a bank), a product line, or a loan, by comparing the financial outcomes (income, profits) to the economic capital required to obtain the outcomes. This is a generic definition, which is used in several variants depending on the specification used to its main elements.

In a simple setting for credit risk modeling, the financial outcomes for a loan can be considered as the revenues that a loan generates (excluding expenses and expected losses) and economic capital can be specified as the capital at risk, i.e., the capital a bank would need to cover its risk exposure in the case of default. In this context, RAROC can be defined as the following ratio:

$$\text{RAROC} = \frac{\text{Loan revenues}}{\text{Capital at risk}}$$

Using RAROC to measure the performance of a loan, a simple decision rule can be formulated: the loan is profitable, if its RAROC exceeds the bank's cost of capital.

The nominator of the RAROC calculation, considers factors such as:

- The spread between the loan rate and the bank's cost of capital (s).
- Fees attributable to the loan (f).
- Expected loan losses (l).
- Operating costs (c).
- Taxation (x).

With these elements, the expected revenues from a loan can be defined as:

$$\text{Loan revenues} = (s + f - l - c)(1 - x)$$

One way to define capital at risk for the calculation of RAROC is to use the change in the value of the loan during the period under consideration (usually 1 year), due to changes in interest rates. For this purpose, the duration of the loan can be used as a measure of the loan's value sensitivity to interest rate changes. More specifically, for a loan of value L, with duration D, and interest rate i, the duration approximation for the change of the loan's value (ΔL) with respect to an interest rate change Δi is:

$$\Delta L \approx -LD\frac{\Delta i}{1 + i}$$

For instance, for a loan with value $L =$ 500,000 €, duration $D = 3$ years, and interest rate $i = 12\%$, an interest rate increase by $\Delta i = 0.02$, will decrease the value of the loan by approximately 26,786 € ($\Delta L = -26{,}786$). This is the amount of risk (i.e., capital at risk) in the denominator of the RAROC calculation. Further, if we assume that there are 0.1% commissions and the spread between the loan's interest rate and the cost of funds is 0.3%, then the annual revenue from the loan is 500,000 (0.004) = 2,000 €. Therefore, the RAROC of this loan is

$$RAROC = \frac{2,000}{26,786} = 7.47\%$$

If the bank's own interest rate is lower than 7.47%, then the loan can be considered as profitable.

This is often referred as a market-based approach. An alternative commonly used approach to define the denominator in the calculation of RAROC when default prediction models are available, is to use the unexpected loan loss:

$$\text{Unexpected loan loss} = \alpha \times LGD \times EAD$$

where LGD and EAD are the loss given default and the exposure, whereas α is a risk factor representing the unexpected default rate. This can be defined through the distribution of historical default rates for loans similar to the one under consideration. For instance, if one assumes that default rates are normally distributed, then at the 99.5% confidence level one can set $\alpha = 2.6\sigma$, where σ is the standard deviation of historical default rates. However, loan loss distributions are usually skewed (i.e., non-normal). To account for this, the standard deviation coefficient in this calculation is often set at higher levels (e.g., 5–6).

1.8 Notes and References

The development of analytical models for financial decision making in the area of credit risk modeling, can be traced back to the work of Altman (1968) on the development of his well-known Z-score model for bankruptcy prediction. During the 1970s, this model was revised (Altman et al. 1977) and other similar models were introduced. An overview of this first period of developments in credit risk measurement was presented by Altman and Saunders (1997).

The option pricing model of Black and Scholes (1973) and the work of Merton (1974) on the pricing of corporate debt, set the basis for the development of structural models. The most well-known implementation of the model of Merton, is the one by Moody's/KMV (Crosbie and Bohn 2003).

Several studies have examined the predictive power of such models in the context of bankruptcy and default prediction, as well as for the prediction of credit ratings. For instance, Hillegeist et al. (2004) found that a structural market model provided significantly better results for predicting bankruptcies as opposed to popular empirical models. Bharath and Shumway (2008) introduced a very simple structural model and concluded that it is useful for predicting defaults when combined with other default predictor variables. Agarwal and Taffler (2008) on the other hand, used a data set of UK bankruptcies and concluded that a structural model does not add much information compared to empirical models. Campbell et al. (2008) also reached a similar conclusion for a sample of bankruptcies in the USA.

In the context of credit risk analysis, Chen and Hill (2013) studied the relationship between different measures of default risk and stock returns. In their comparison between default models and the ratings of Moody's and S&P for a sample of UK, they found an empirical z-score model to have a stronger correlation to the ratings of the two agencies compared to two structural models, thus leading the authors to note that "this suggests a relatively high reliance on accounting ratios in the default risk assessments of the rating agencies". On the other hand, Doumpos et al. (2015) used the probability of default estimates from the Merton model as a predictor of credit ratings for European companies and found that although it adds significant information compared to standard financial data, it does not offer much compared to other market data, namely capitalization. Some applications of structural models to non-listed companies and consumer loans were presented by Niklis et al. (2014) and Thomas (2009).

Reduced form model were pioneered by Jarrow and Turnbull (1992, 1995) who presented models of default and recovery rates using a Poisson process. Similar models have been presented in several other works, with the model of Duffie and Singleton (1999) being one of the most well-known. Several studies have also presented the fitting of reduced form models to historical data, usually based on hazard models (Bharath and Shumway 2008; Campbell et al. 2008; Chava and Jarrow 2004) and provide empirical results on the performance of such models over structural models. In most cases, the reduced form approaches were found to provide superior results. An overview of different reduced form models, their implementations, and empirical results can be found in the works of Anson et al. (2008) and van Deventer et al. (2013, Chap. 6).

Chapter 2
Credit Scoring and Rating

2.1 Introduction

As explained in the previous chapter, credit risk modeling and assessment involves three key elements: (1) probability of default (PD), (2) exposure at default (EAD), and (3) loss given default (LGD). In this book, we shall focus on approaches for PD estimation and the specification of the creditworthiness of corporate and consumer borrowers. In Sect. 1.6, three types of approaches were identified, including judgmental, data-driven, and financial models. For the presentation in this book, we shall concentrate on data-driven approaches, which are the most general and widely used for credit risk assessment and management.

Data-driven approaches for credit risk analysis are based on scoring and rating models and systems. Credit scoring and rating both refer to the process of quantifying the level of credit risk for a borrower (obligor), taking into consideration all the available information that is related to the borrower's ability and willingness to repay a debt obligation based on the agreed terms.

Although scoring and rating approaches provide credit risk assessments, they are often considered in slightly different context. Credit scoring usually refers to models and systems that provide a numerical credit score for each borrower. The credit score is an indicator of the borrower's creditworthiness and probability of default. On the other hand, the main output of credit rating is a risk rating expressed on an ordinal qualitative scale. Each risk grade is associated to an empirically estimated PD that describes all borrowers who are assigned to that grade. Credit ratings are typically used for corporate loans, bond issues, and countries (e.g., sovereign credit ratings), and often they are publicly available. On the other hand, credit scores are solely for internal use by financial institutions and corporate clients. Finally, it is worth noting that although credit scoring is based on automated analytical models, credit rating may involve a combination of analytical and judgmental assessments, thus relying on a more elaborate and in-depth process.

M. Doumpos et al., *Analytical Techniques in the Assessment of Credit Risk*, EURO Advanced Tutorials on Operational Research,
https://doi.org/10.1007/978-3-319-99411-6_2

Credit scoring and rating is a fundamental ingredient of credit risk management. Such models are not simply used to support the decision-making process for loan approval. In addition, they are used for loan pricing and credit portfolio management, which refers to the assessment of the risk exposure for a whole portfolio of loans. The implementation of credit scoring and rating systems makes it much easier to monitor over time the risk exposure derived either from a single loan or from a loan portfolio. Moreover, they facilitate the reporting process (internally as well as external reporting to supervisory authorities) and provide an analytical mechanism for target setting in terms of capital requirements, which are needed to cover expected/unexpected losses, and customer relationship management.

Thus, the main benefits derived by the implementation of credit scoring and rating systems, can be outlined as follows:

1. Reduction of the subjectivity in the loan evaluation process.
2. Enabling analytical credit risk management, including scenario analysis and stress testing.
3. Promoting consistency and transparency, through a common framework for the evaluation of all customers.
4. Reduction of the time and cost needed for loan appraisal.

Credit scoring and rating models can be developed either internally by a credit institution or provided by external vendors. Internal models are used by credit institutions such as banks, who have access to the historical data needed for developing and calibrating the models to their specific credit portfolio. External models are typically developed by credit rating agencies, credit bureaus, and consultancy companies, and their outputs are provided to users, including credit institutions, corporate clients, and investors. For instance, investors use external credit ratings to assess the risk of bonds issued by firms and countries, whereas firms use external ratings to assess the creditworthiness of their customers. Studies have shown that even though external credit ratings are not as powerful for predicting defaults as internal or financial models, they are good indicators of systematic risk (i.e., the risk due to external market shocks). Moreover, external ratings are also used for benchmarking and reviewing internal models. Overall, it is worth noting that relying on a single credit scoring and rating system (internal or external) may not be the best option. Instead, using models developed in different contexts and with diverse input information, may lead to a more comprehensive analysis of credit risk.

Taking into consideration the above mentioned underlying differences between credit scoring and rating systems, this chapter will describe the basic characteristics of both schemes. Before that, we first discuss different application contexts and scoring/rating types, and then proceed with the analysis of the modeling requirements and the modeling process. The chapter closes with a brief discussion of the credit rating industry, focusing on the major credit rating agencies.

2.2 The Contexts of Credit Scoring and Rating Systems

Credit scoring and credit systems/models are constructed and implemented in a wide range of different contexts and variants, depending on the target goals and area of use. Below we outline four aspects that distinguish between different types of scoring and rating systems, depending on their scope of application. These involve the time frame of risk assessment, the entities being evaluated, the nature of the assessment, as well as the emerging area of social lending.

2.2.1 *Through the Cycle and Point in Time Assessments*

The existing regulatory framework, as set by the Basel Committee on Banking Supervision, distinguishes two types of credit rating philosophies, namely through the cycle and point in time.

Through the cycle assessments are primarily of interest for major credit rating agencies. Through the cycle credit risk assessment have a long-term orientation covering at least one business cycle, rather than short-term estimates. Therefore, such assessments are robust to short-term changes and they are subject to less frequent updates.

On the other hand, point in time assessments, are usually employed by internal systems developed by credit institutions and banks. A point in time analysis focuses on the current and short-term condition of a borrower, in a predefined period, which does not extend a period more than one year, in most cases. These ratings are more volatile, and they are updated in a timely manner to reflect any new information regarding the status of the borrower. For the above reasons point in time assessments are used in cases involving short-term transactions and loans.

In terms of predictive power and accuracy of these two approaches, the findings from existing research are mixed. Therefore, the choice between these two types of assessments, depends mostly on the scope and requirements of the analysis. Moreover, it must be also noted that while credit risk and default are easier to define in a point in time context (e.g., default during a period of 1 year), the extension to a through the cycle framework is not an easy task, because the time until default should be explicitly defined and modeled analytically.

2.2.2 *Issuer Ratings and Issue-Specific Ratings*

An issuer credit rating is a forward-looking opinion about an obligor's creditworthiness. Issuer credit ratings could be either long-term or short-term, depending the examined scope. There are different forms of issuer credit ratings, such as counterparty credit ratings, corporate credit ratings and sovereign credit ratings. There is plethora of reasons for an issuer to obtain such a rating. The most common refers to access in capital markets or other funding. For instance, a company which is ranked at the top level of the rating scale, has a good history of repaying its debt and low risk of default. This is an asset for the firm and can be used either to improve its access to financing (lower interest rates, easy access to external financing) and strengthen its relationship with various stakeholders (better agreements with suppliers, attract investors, etc.).

Apart from issuer ratings there are also issue-specific ratings. In contrast to issuer ratings that involve the creditworthiness of an entity, an issue-specific rating is an opinion about the creditworthiness of an obligor with respect to a specific financial obligation (e.g., a specific loan). An issue-specific assessment considers the terms of a loan, such as its duration, the collaterals, the uses of the loan (e.g., for mortgages the value of the house), and other information regarding the risk profile of a specific debt issue.

2.2.3 Behavioral and Profit Scoring

Behavioral scoring applies to consumer lending and refers to risk of a customer depending on his/her observed behavior. This involves mostly existing customers, for which data are available. Behavioral scores are short-term assessments and they are frequently updated (usually monthly), based on all available information (e.g., account balances, changes in employment status, missed payments). Thus, in contrast to the static nature of standard credit scores and ratings, which focus on the assessment of new customers based on application data, behavioral scores dynamically monitor the payment and purchase behavior of existing customers and provide updated default risk estimates. Moreover, behavioral scores are used for setting of credit limits, managing debt collection, as well as for marketing purposes (e.g., offering new credit and financing products to customers).

In contrast to credit and behavioral scoring which focus on risk assessment, profit scoring emphasizes on the likelihood that granting credit to a customer will be profitable or not. Profit scoring extends traditional models adopting a broader perspective that incorporates marketing, pricing, and operation decisions, in addition to typical credit risk assessment and default prediction models. There are different types of profit scoring, including account-level and customer-level models. Account-level profit scoring calculates the profit from a specific account. It focuses on a specific financial product, ignoring relationships and effects that may exist due to the presence of different financial products belonging to one customer. Customer-level profit scoring covers all the available accounts of a customer. This could give a better outlook for customer's profile and could be used for the promotion of new financial products.

2.2.4 *Social Lending*

With the emerge of new advances in financial technology (FinTech), new financing channels have been introduced for corporations and individual customers. Among them, peer-to-peer (P2P) lending, also known as social lending, has become quite popular. P2P lending relies on online platforms that enable direct transactions between borrowers and lenders without the presence of a financial institution, thus providing easier access to credit compared to bank lending. Such platforms first appeared in the mid-2000s in UK (Zopa in 2005) and USA (Prosper in 2006) and they have grown rapidly. For instance, recent data from P2P Finance Association show a rapid increase in the size of the P2P lending market in the UK, from £2.16 billion at the end of 2014 to almost £8.5 billion in the first quarter of 2017 (with more than £5.1 billion referring to business lending). Similar reports for the USA, indicate that the size of the US P2P lending market currently exceeds $68 billion.

Credit risk modeling for social lending platforms is an emerging topic of major interest, as the P2P market remains mostly unregulated and not supervised in the way traditional financial institutions are. Moreover, it should be noted that default risk is generally higher in P2P lending platforms compared to traditional lending and P2P loans lack collateral and guarantees. Thus, credit scoring and rating models are very useful in this area but need adjustments to the special features of P2P lending to cover the needs of investors, lenders and borrowers. Among others, the handling of big data and transparency are important issues, given the wealth of information collected from online sources about potential borrowers as well as the need to promote transparency for all parties involved in online lending (lenders and borrowers).

2.3 Modeling Requirements

The development and use of credit scoring and rating models, is governed by regulatory requirements imposed by local and international supervisors, such as central banks. Before we describe the model development process, we present below the basic specifications of a credit scoring and rating system, as outlined by the Basel's Committee rules.

1. Meaningful differentiation of risk. A credit rating system must be primarily designed to distinguish risk rather than to minimize regulatory capital requirements. The grades of the rating system must be properly defined to represent different levels of credit risk. In addition, borrowers within the same grade must be treated differently according to their transaction's characteristics. Finally, the exposures must be meaningfully distributed across grades preventing excessive concentration in any particular grade.

2. Continuous evaluation of borrowers. All borrowers and loans in a credit portfolio should be, at a minimum, annually re-rated, taking into consideration all new information about a borrowers' status and progress.
3. Oversight of the system's operation. The operation of a credit scoring/rating system must be constantly monitored for its proper functioning and correctness. In addition, the system must be subjected to sufficient and efficient controls (i.e. stress tests) and an adequate feedback mechanism between the responsible parties should exist to ensure the system's integrity.
4. Correct selection of risk assessment attributes. The developers should be able to demonstrate that the creditworthiness of the borrowers can be properly analyzed based on the risk factors and attributes considered by the credit scoring and rating systems. The analysis should be based on the future performance of a borrower based on currently available information about the borrower and the external environment.
5. Collecting a substantial data base. The database used for the development and the evaluation of a credit rating system must be representative of reality. It must incorporate historical data on the characteristics of the borrowers', past credit scores, ratings, and PD estimations, credit migrations data, payments history etc.

2.4 Development Process

Having in mind the specifications described above, the development of credit scoring and rating models is a complex and data intensive process that requires both judgmental expertise by the analysts as well as technical sophistication. An outline of the process is illustrated in Fig. 2.1, whereas the following subsections discuss all the main steps in more detail.

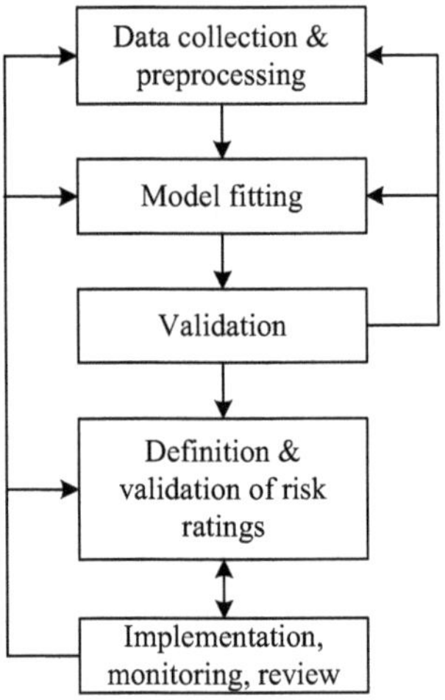

Fig. 2.1 The process for developing credit risk scoring and rating models

2.4.1 Data Collection and Pre-processing

Once the goals and context of the credit model are set, the process begins with the collection of appropriate data for model building. The outcome of the data collection and preprocessing phase is a data set X consisting of m cases (each corresponding to a borrower or loan), which can be described as pairs $\{\mathbf{x}_i, y_i\}_{i=1}^{m}$, where $\mathbf{x}_i = (x_{i1}, x_{i2}, \ldots, x_{in})$ is the input attribute vector describing the characteristics of case i on n risk attributes, and y_i is the known status of this case (i.e., defaulted, non-defaulted).

In a typical setting, data for defaulted and non-defaulted cases are collected. The group of cases in default usually consists of borrowers with overdue payments by at least 90 days, but this definition of default depends on the context of each particular credit institution and the uses of the credit model. The main input data can be obtained through various sources. For instance, credit institutions use their internal historical databases, but external sources can be used, too. At this stage, some preprocessing of the data is necessary to transform them into meaningful risk attributes, eliminate outliers, and select the appropriate set of attributes for the analysis. Algorithmic procedures and statistical tests can be used to assess the information value and discriminating power of the attributes under consideration. However, expert judgment is also very useful at this stage to select meaningful credit risk rating attributes, that not only have discriminating ability, but they also make business sense.

The type of input data and predictor variables used for credit scoring and rating, varies depending on the application context. Typically, a mixture of "hard" quantitative attributes and "soft" qualitative data is used to describe the creditworthiness of a borrower. One important issue that credit analysts should bear in mind when considering qualitative information, is that subjectivity should be kept to a minimum and ensure that qualitative data are handled in a consistent manner throughout all stages of data collection and processing.

The risk assessment process for consumer loans relies on information about the income of the borrower, his/her assets, existing loan payments and payment history, the borrower's family, social and employment status, collaterals and guarantees, as well as the type and purpose of the loan (e.g., credit card, mortgage loan, etc.).

On the other hand, corporate credit risk models, typically consider data such as:

- financial/accounting information,
- behavioral and transaction data,
- size and age,
- market conditions and competitive advantages,
- stock market data (for listed companies),
- corporate governance,
- corporate news and analytics,
- the external environment (business sector data, regional and country-level information).

Below we provide a discussion of these factors.

2.4.1.1 Financial Data

Financial information is derived from corporate financial statements, which are publicly available, i.e., the balance sheet, income statement, and cash flow statement. Typically, financial ratios are constructed by combining accounting data to derive meaningful indicators of all aspects of the financial strength of a firm, including profitability, solvency, liquidity, and management efficiency:

- Profitability ratios measure the ability of the firm to use its assets and capital in an efficient manner for generating profits. Popular ratios in this category are return on assets, return on equity, and profit margins (gross, operating, and net profit margin).
- Solvency ratios focus on measuring the debt burden of a firm, with ratios such as debt to assets, debt to equity, and interest coverage (operating income to interest expenses), being typical indicators of the extent to which a firm relies on external financing (debt) for its operations.
- Liquidity represents the ability of a company to cover its short-term financing needs by matching its assets to liabilities (current assets versus current liabilities). Typical ratios in this category include working capital (current assets-current liabilities) to total assets, the current ratio (current assets/current liabilities), and the quick ratio (current assets excluding inventories/current liabilities).
- Finally, management efficiency refers to the operational performance of the firm in converting different types assets into cash and sales, as well as the management of the credit it receives from its suppliers. Typical ratios in this dimension include the turnover of inventories (cost of sales/inventories), receivables (sales/accounts receivable), payables (cost of sales/accounts payable), and total assets (sales/total assets).

While such financial ratios are typically examined in a static setting using the most recent available data at the time a loan application is examined, growth indicators are also relevant, providing a dynamic view of the status of a firm. Usually, these focus on sales and operations growth (in value and volume) over a period of 3–5 years.

2.4.1.2 Behavioral and Transaction Data

The financial data outlined above provide fundamental indications about the financial status and strength of a corporate borrower. Transaction data, on the other hand, cover the daily operations of a firm and its daily business transactions with its creditors (e.g., supplies and banks), focusing on payment history data. Such behavioral indicators involve information such as credit limits, current balances, and delinquencies, among others, which are monitored and updated much more regularly than accounting data from financial statements, thus providing a more dynamic view of the creditworthiness status of a borrower.

2.4.1.3 Size and Age

In addition to the above financial and behavioral data, several studies have found that corporate defaults are often related to the size and age of a company. On the one hand, large companies usually have easier access to cheaper financing either from credit institutions or the financial markets (e.g., through bond issues), while also being able to achieve better credit terms from suppliers and other creditors. On the other hand, small and new companies are more vulnerable to adverse conditions and often lack access to finance, which is important during the first stages of a company. Moreover, historical information is often not available for such companies, thus making credit decisions and risk assessments more challenging. Regarding the size of a company, different measures can be employed. The most common ones involve total assets and revenues, whereas market capitalization can also be used for listed companies.

2.4.1.4 Market Conditions and Competitive Advantages

A key element for the assessment of the prospects of a company is the knowledge of the conditions prevailing in the market in it which operates. Market conditions are constantly changing, and these changes affect the operation of a firm. The main elements to be considered are:

- The level of competition in the market (e.g., number and size of competing firms, market shares).
- The openness of the market and existing regulations that affect competition and the operation of the market.
- Market outlook, trends and prospects.

In the context of the prevailing market conditions, competitive advantages that a firm possesses are of major importance. These may include advantages in terms of technology development and adoption, research and development advantages, innovation, special advantages in the supply chain, as well as operations and product diversification.

Moreover, the network of the firm is also an important issue. The status of major suppliers and customers of a firm directly affects its performance and viability. Firms relying too much on suppliers/customers of low creditworthiness are likely to face difficulties due to risks that naturally mitigate through their business network.

2.4.1.5 Financial Markets Data

A common criticism of accounting-based data such as the ones described earlier, is that they are static and backward looking (i.e., they reflect the past performance of a firm, rather than its prospects). Stock market data overcome these limitations for publicly traded (listed) firms. Stock prices embody all information available to market participants and investors about the status and prospects of a firm. Market data, which have been found to be relevant for credit risk assessment, include the volatility of stock returns, market capitalization, and valuation ratios (price/earnings ratio, book to market value, earnings per share, etc.). The Black-Scholes-Merton structural model, which was described in Sect. 1.6.3, is a well-known example of a model that relies on market data for default risk estimation. Previous studies have shown, that market data are more applicable for short- term periods and accounting data for medium or long-term period.

2.4.1.6 Corporate Governance

While financial and market data are commonly used in corporate credit scoring and rating, recent practices and research have also focused on additional non-financial data. A popular emerging trend involves the consideration of corporate governance information, which relates to management practices and business ethics. Corporate scandals like the failures of Enron, WorldCom, and Lehman Brothers, have brought governance practices into the spotlight of academic research.

Corporate governance cover issues related to the composition and structure of the board of directors, the competence and background of top executives (e.g., chairman, chief executive officer, chief financial officer, etc.), the transparency and accountability in the decision-making process, and the protection of shareholder rights, among others. Several studies have shown that such issues are positively related to corporate performance and financial strength. Thus, incorporating them into credit rating models adds valuable information on the long-term stability of and soundness of corporate clients in credit risk modeling.

Corporate governance enhances the examination of traditional management and organizational aspects, such as the qualifications, experience, and competence of the management team, management style, corporate culture, business planning, the implementation of internal audit and control procedures, human resources and customer relationship management, etc.

2.4.1.7 Corporate News and Analytics

Finally, a recent trend focuses on using information about corporate news gathered from various online sources, including social networks. The wealth of information available online is a new opportunity for credit scoring and rating, not only for corporate loans but also for consumer credit. Such information enhances traditional analytical models with non-financial data about the operation of companies, their status in the market, their strategic planning (e.g., mergers and acquisitions), as well as their relationship with customers and suppliers (i.e., the business network of a company). The vast volume of such data creates new challenges for feature extraction with new technologies, such as text and social network analytics, thus leading to big data systems.

2.4.2 Model Fitting

The second stage involves the model fitting process, which refers to the identification of the model's parameters that best describe (fit) the training data. For instance, assume the following linear model:

$$f(\mathbf{x}) = \beta_0 + \beta_1 x_1 + \beta_2 x_2 + \cdots + \beta_n x_n$$

where the vector $\boldsymbol{\beta} = (\beta_0, \beta_1, \ldots, \beta_n)$ includes the constant term β_0 and coefficients $\beta_1, \ldots, \beta_n$ for the risk rating attributes. With such a model, the fitting process should provide the best (optimal) estimates for the elements of $\boldsymbol{\beta}$, based on the information provided by the training data. This can be expressed as an optimization problem of the following general form:

$$\boldsymbol{\beta}^* = \arg\min_{\boldsymbol{\beta}\in\mathbb{R}} L(\boldsymbol{\beta}, X) \tag{2.1}$$

where $\boldsymbol{\beta}^*$ denotes the optimal parameter vector and L is a loss function measuring the differences between the model's output and the given classification of the training cases.

It should be noted that problem (2.1) is an empirical proxy of the true problem. The true objective is to minimize the loss from the application of the credit model to any borrower. However, as the population of borrowers in not available (and changes over time), the empirical loss problem (2.1) provides a reasonable basis for model construction. In fact, problem (2.1) is a regression-like problem, with the only difference being that the dependent variable is binary (default/non-default) as opposed to continuous in standard regression models.

The optimization problem (2.1) can be expressed in several analytical forms, including, among others, unconstraint optimization, linear, and non-linear programming, depending on the general form of the prediction model, and the choice of the loss function.

On the algorithmic side, several analytical methodologies and approaches can be used for model fitting, including statistical, data mining, and operations research techniques. The next chapter will describe some commonly used approaches, their advantages and limitations.

2.4.3 Model Validation

The model derived from the above training process should be validated against a sample different from the one used for model fitting. This secondary sample is referred to as the validation or holdout sample. The validation sample involves the same risk attributes used to fit the model, but it involves different cases (borrowers/loans) from the ones included in the training set. The objective of the validation exercise is to assess the expected predictive performance of the model in a context that resembles the actual use of the model in practice. A variety of performance measures are used at this stage, including statistical as well as economic measures (see Sect. 3.3). If the validation results are unsatisfactory, then either the model fitting process should be repeated (e.g., with a different algorithmic approach) or the process should re-start from the data processing phase (e.g., selecting a different set of risk attributes, adding new data, etc.). Generally, the three first phases (data preparation, model fitting, and validation) require multiple iterations until a satisfactory outcome is achieved.

An important part of the validation process involves the analysis of the performance of the model in terms of the quality and robustness of its results. The most common evaluation scheme involves the evaluation of the model in a back-testing context. Back-testing refers to the statistical evaluation of the generalizing and predictive ability of a credit model using historical data different from the ones used for constructing the model. To this end, out-of-sample and out-of-time tests are performed.

Out-of-sample tests involve the application of a credit model to borrowers not included in the sample used to build the model. Although out-of-sample testing is standard in statistical model building, the time dimension cannot be overlooked when it comes to evaluating the performance of credit risk models. Typically, such models are developed at some specific point in time and then they are used in future time periods, until they are updated. Thus, model testing on borrowers different from the ones considered for model development is not enough. Instead, the robustness of the model over time needs to be verified, too.

This issue is addressed with out-of-time tests, which refer to the application of a credit model to data from a different time period than the one considered during model development. For instance, a credit model is developed using historical data up to a period t and its performance is assessed to subsequent time periods $t + 1, t + 2, \ldots$ Ideally, out-of-sample and out-of-time tests should be combined to obtain more reliable estimates for the true performance of credit risk assessment models in realistic cases. In this context, the validation of a model is performed using data involving different borrowers and time periods from the ones considered during model fitting.

Even in this way, however, a single test may not yield convincing results about the predictive ability of a credit scoring/rating model, as a good performance on a specific time period and sample of borrowers may not be indicative of the true performance in other instances. Walk-forward testing is a common approach used to

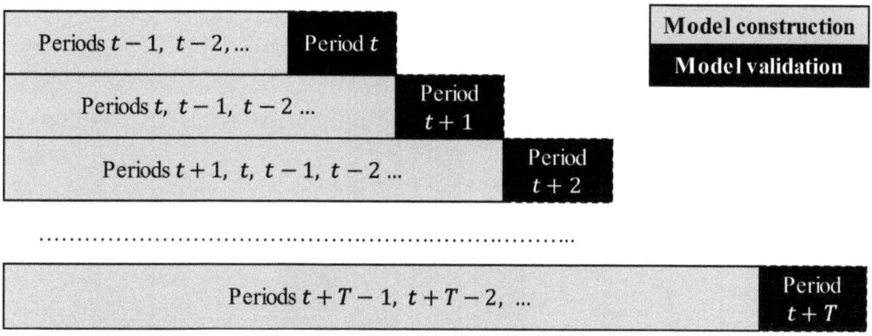

Fig. 2.2 Walk-forward testing approach

overcome such difficulties and reduce the likelihood of having biased results due to the chosen test sample and period. Under a walk-forward scheme, the adopted credit risk modeling approach is tested over $T + 1$ consecutive runs, as illustrated in Fig. 2.2. Starting from a time period t, past historical data up to period $t - 1$ are used for model construction. The developed model is tested on a sample of borrowers for period t. Then, the time-window is moved one period ahead and the process is repeated by constructing a new model using data up to t and testing the model to borrowers in period $t + 1$. The same process is repeated over multiple time periods, thus leading to more reliable and robust assessments. This process can be further enhanced with resampling techniques (cross-validation, bootstrap) to further reduce the dependency on particular test samples and enable the statistical analysis of the results.

An alternative to back-testing model validation is benchmarking, which refers to the comparison of a credit model's results to those of external assessments. Back-testing relies on statistical methods to compare the estimates derived by credit scoring and rating models against realized outcomes. Benchmarking, on the other hand, focuses on comparisons against results from external sources, such as ratings issued by credit rating agencies. Benchmarking tests facilitate the identification of reasons to review and calibrate internally developed rating models. In contrast to the statistical nature of back-testing validation, benchmarking is based on a rather qualitative and judgmental procedure. The objective of such tests is not to ensure that a given credit scoring/rating reproduces external benchmarks in an accurate manner. Instead, the goal is to identify significant discrepancies and analyze the reasons behind them. Discrepancies may naturally arise because external benchmarks and internal credit scoring/rating models are not developed based on the same goals and customer base. However, the observed discrepancies may also be indications that an internal model requires calibration and improvements. Of course, in implementing such comparative analyses, the proper selection of the benchmark is crucial to ensure that meaningful results can be obtained. In Sect. 2.5 we briefly describe the credit rating of major rating agencies, which are commonly used for benchmarking purposes, at least for corporate credit ratings.

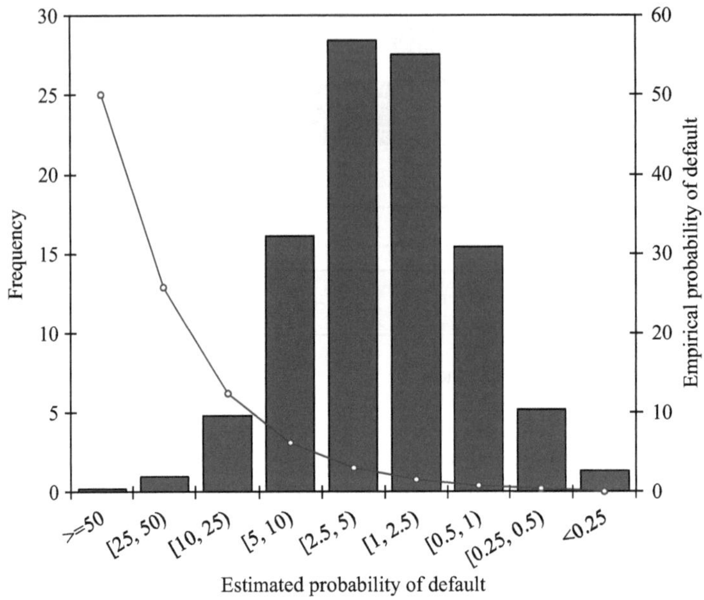

Fig. 2.3 Credit risk ratings and probabilities of default

2.4.4 Definition and Validation of Ratings

In the context of credit rating, once the model is judged satisfactory through the above validation process, the derived credit scores should be mapped to risk rating classes. Usually, at least ten rating categories are defined providing a refined categorization of the risk level of the borrowers. The rating grades are constructed considering various issues. For instance, each rating class should be associated to empirical PD estimates that are well diversified between neighboring categories and the distribution of the borrowers across the risk categories should not have excessive concentration of cases in specific risk grades.

An illustrative example is shown in Fig. 2.3, where the PD estimated through a credit scoring model is used to define nine risk grades, ranging from low risk (PD $<$ 0.25%) to high risk borrowers (PD$\geq$50%). The distribution (frequency) of a sample of borrowers in the risk grades is also shown, together with the corresponding empirical PDs. For each risk grade, the empirical PD is defined by the ratio between the number of defaulted borrowers in that risk grade to the total number of borrowers in the risk grade. It is evident that there is no excess concentration of borrowers in the risk grades (the two middle categories have less than 30% of the cases). Moreover, the empirical PD rises by about a factor of two as we move from low risk grades to high risk ones. This indicates a good differentiation of risk between the categories. Finally, it is worth noting that the empirical PD closely matches the estimated PD ranges that are shown in the horizontal axis of the graph for each risk category, thus indicating that the calibration of the ratings is in accordance with the estimations of the risk scoring model.

Similarly to model validation, the rating scheme should also be validated in terms of its stability over time (e.g., ratings migration), the distribution of the borrowers in the rating groups, and the consistency between the estimated probabilities of default in each group and the empirical ones which are taken from the population of rated borrowers. If the validation of the derived ratings does not yield satisfactory results, a different specification of the ratings should be first considered, whereas the construction of a new model would be the last option.

2.4.5 Implementation

The last stage of the whole process involves the implementation of the outcomes into a credit scoring/rating system that will be used to derive real time credit risk estimates for all new loan applications. The results and performance of the system are under frequent monitoring and review, and updates are performed either by re-calibrating the ratings (without altering the decision model), or by re-estimating a new model, when there is a significant and consistent degradation in the quality and accuracy of the obtained risk estimates.

2.5 Credit Rating Agencies

Credit rating agencies (CRAs) provide individual and institutional investors with information that assists them in determining whether issuers of debt obligations and fixed-income securities will be able to meet their obligations. The debt instruments rated by CRAs include government bonds, corporate bonds, certificates of deposits, municipal bonds, preferred stock, and collateralized securities, such as mortgage-backed securities and collateralized debt obligations. The role of CRAs is crucial due to the globalization of the financial markets and the wide range of debt issues, which pose challenges to their monitoring and risk assessment for investors, financial institutions, supervisors, and other stakeholders.

CRAs have a long history that dates to the early 1900s. Currently, there are three leading CRAs, namely Moody's, Standard and Poor's (S&P), and Fitch, which dominate the global market with a market share of more than 90%. Moody's and S&P are the two largest agencies, each covering about 40% of the global market. Fitch covers approximately 15% of the market, with approximately 350,000 outstanding ratings. Many other smaller and specialized CRAs operate in local markets and countries.

CRAs provide ratings for corporate and sovereign debt using multi-grade schemes, that range from top rated issuers (low credit risk) to cases in default. The ratings are expressed in an ordinal scale. An example of the main risk grades used in

Table 2.1 Rating categories by Moody's, Standard & Poor's, and Fitch

Category	Moody's	S&P/ Fitch	Description
Investment grades	Aaa	AAA	Highly recommended. Small risk of default. Stable investment.
	Aa	AA	High quality investment. Slightly higher level of long-term risk.
	A	A	High-medium quality investment. Vulnerable to economic changes.
	Baa	BBB	Medium quality. Quite secure at present, with risk problems in long-term period.
Speculative grades	Ba	BB	Medium quality. Not well secured investment
	B	B	Quite secure in present. Likely to default in the future.
	Caa	CCC	Poor quality. High likelihood of default
	Ca	CC	Highly speculative investment. Close to default.
		C	Low quality. High likelihood of default. Still paying at present.
	C	D	In default.

Table 2.2 Historical average one-year default rates (in %) by rating grade

Moody's (1920–2016)		S&P (1982–2016)		Fitch (1990–2014)	
Aaa	0.00	AAA	0.00	AAA	0.00
Aa	0.02	AA	0.02	AA	0.00
A	0.05	A	0.06	A	0.03
Baa	0.17	BBB	0.18	BBB	0.17
Ba	0.91	BB	0.72	BB	0.82
B	3.39	B	3.76	B	2.53
Caa	8.38	CCC/C	26.78	CCC/C	28.13
Ca-C	25.62				

Sources: Moody's Annual Default Study: Corporate Default and Recovery Rates, 1920–2016
S&P: https://goo.gl/kT3Nio, Fitch: https://goo.gl/fRAAMb

the ratings of Moody's, S&P, and Fitch is shown in Table 2.1. As shown in the table, two major sets of grades can be identified, namely investment and speculative grades. Investment grades correspond to low risk borrowers. Historically, data provided by the CRAs indicate that the one-year default rates for investment grades are lower than 0.2%, on average. Speculative grades, on the other hand correspond to borrowers of low creditworthiness and high default risk. Defaults are also included in the low-end of the rating scales. As shown in Table 2.2, historically, the one-year default rates for borrowers with speculative ratings, range from 0.7% for the high end of the range of speculative grades (i.e., Ba/BB ratings), up to more than 25% for the highest risk grades (i.e., C and D).

Ratings are defined for different time periods. Short-term credit ratings measure credit risk over a short time period (typically one year) and reflect a debtor's ability to fulfill his short-term financial obligations. For longer periods we refer to medium- and long-term ratings. Rating agencies may adopt different rating scales for ratings of different horizons.

Credit ratings issued by major CRAs combine analytical and judgmental approaches and consider a wide range of different input data, such as the ones described earlier in Sect. 2.4.1. The data are collected through proprietary databases and industry/market reports, as well as through onsite meetings of expert rating analysts with executives of the rated companies.

Despite their widespread use by investors, financial/credit institutions, regulators and supervisory agencies, as well as non-financial corporations, CRAs' ratings have received much criticism, mainly on issues such as:

- Lack of transparency and accountability, conflict of interest: the way CRAs prepare their risk ratings is generally not publicly disclosed, thus raising questions on the practices being followed. Moreover, the fact that CRAs revenues depend on the fees paid by the entities being rated, raises further concerns about possible conflicts of interest between the raters and those rated.
- Promoting debt explosion: credit risk scoring and rating enhanced the risk management practices of financial and credit institutions, leading to better risk estimates, thus enabling banks and other credit institutions to lower their risk premiums and reduce the cost of debt financing. As a result, debt is now more accessible for firms and consumers, but this may contribute to increasing systemic risk due to credit bubble and crunches.
- Poor predictive ability: with the outbreak of the global credit crisis of 2007–2008 and the failure of CRAs to predict major corporate failures (Lehman Brothers, Enron, WorldCom, etc.), the predictive ability of CRAs ratings have been put in question. This criticism is supported by several empirical studies that have found CRAs' ratings to be weaker predictors of corporate default compared to commonly used accounting and market-based default prediction models and risk scoring/rating systems developed internally by financial institutions.
- Pro-cyclicality: CRAs claim that their rates are through the cycle (cf. Sect. 2.2.1), that is their ratings are independent of the state of the business cycle, representing the true underlying credit risk of the rated borrower. However, some critics have noted that the ratings were too optimistic during periods of economic growth and too pessimistic during recessionary times, thus indicating pro-cyclical behavior. Such a behavior puts further questions on the information value of credit ratings and the role in the exacerbating crisis conditions.

Despite the criticisms, credit ratings issued by CRAs are widely regarded as integral parts of risk management systems throughout the business world. Of course, decisions about credit risk management are not solely driven by CRAs' ratings. Instead, such ratings complement other approaches and systems, thus facilitating the implementation of integrated risk management systems, as credit risk is a multifaceted issue and one risk measure may not be enough to adequately describe all factors that affect the creditworthiness of a borrower and the risk of a loan portfolio. From that point of view, the ratings of CRAs can be particularly useful to describe some components of systematic risk as evident by the way the affect credit risk products, such as credit spreads.

2.6 Notes and References

Credit scoring and rating, except for its technical and modeling aspects, has received much attention among researchers and practitioners, on several other issues.

One of the most fundamental is related to the information value and the effects of credit scoring and rating, for investors, corporations, and consumers. Mester (1997) provides an overview of the uses of credit scoring by the banking sector in the USA, for consumer and business loans, and discusses a number of benefits, limitations and challenges. Einav et al. (2013) studied the adoption of credit scoring by an auto finance company and found that it led to a major improvement in profitability, reducing lending to high-risk applicants, and promoting consistency across the company's network. Other studies have focused on small business lending. For instance, Frame et al. (2001) found that the adoption of credit scoring systems at US banks promoted small-business lending by reducing information costs between lenders and borrowers, which reduces the value of traditional local bank lending relationships. Similar results have also been reported in other US-based studies (Berger et al. 2005, 2011). On the other hand, the number of studies for Europe or other areas is more limited. However, in a recent study Forcella (2015) surveyed 58 European microfinance institutions and found that more than half are ready to use credit scoring systems.

Validation schemes (out-of-sample, out-of-time) and validation procedure is an important and difficult task in credit risk assessment. In order to obtain accurate results proper training and validation data sets should be created. Sobehart et al. (2000), analyze the steps of a validation methodology. More information about benchmarking and back-testing techniques can be found in the report of the Basel Committee on Banking Supervision (2005).

The literature is also rich about the role and importance of credit ratings, which are mostly relevant for large firms. Kisgen (2006, 2009) provides empirical evidence showing that credit ratings affect capital structure decisions, particularly when there is a change in the ratings. Firms that are downgraded reduce their debt, whereas upgrades do not affect subsequent capital structure activity, thus suggesting that firms have rating targets. In another study, Almeida et al. (2017) examined the connections between corporate investments and sovereign ratings, which define a ceiling for corporate credit ratings, and concluded that firms reduce investments and credit market exposure following sovereign rating downgrades. Further details about the status the credit rating industry, its contributions/failures, and main criticisms, can be found in several works, such as those of Frost (2007), Bolton et al. (2012), Jeon and Lovo (2013), and Tichy et al. (2011). Overall, even though there seems to be a consensus in academic research that credit ratings, as provided by major CRAs are not as powerful predictors of default as special default prediction models based on empirical and financial approaches, they do contribute to credit risk management, enabling the consideration of credit risk in an integrated manner. For instance, a recent study by Hilscher and Wilson (2017) provides evidence showing that credit ratings are strong indicators of systematic risk.

Other issues related to credit scoring/rating and its uses and applications in various contexts, including behavioral and profit scoring, fraud detection, risk-based pricing, social lending, etc., can be found in the works of Thomas et al. (2002), Van Gestel and Baesens (2009), Emekter et al. (2015), Serrano-Cinca and Gutiérrez-Nieto (2016), Lemonakis et al. (2015), and Lemonakis et al. (2017).

Chapter 3
Data Analytics for Developing and Validating Credit Models

3.1 Introduction

According to the methodological framework analyzed in the previous chapter, the development of credit risk assessment model in the context of credit scoring and rating, is used considered as regression-like problem, which is standard in areas such as statistics and data mining/machine learning. This is data intensive task that involves a considerable level of sophistication in terms of data preparation, analysis, and modeling. Data analytics is an area that has evolved from different disciplines, including statistics, computer science, and operations research. Data analytics is involved with all aspects of data analysis, knowledge discovery, and data modeling, for decision making in a descriptive and predictive context.

From a data analytics perspective, the construction of credit scoring and rating models can be considered as a classification task. Classification refers to the assignment of a set of objects or observations to predefined categories. In the context of credit risk analysis, this involves the classification of borrowers to predefined categories (classes), which correspond to different levels of credit risk.

The main input in this setting is a set of (historical) data that include defaulted (D) and non-defaulted (ND) borrowers. This binary (dichotomic) setting is convenient, because it is based on a well-defined and "objective" definition of default. For instance, loans with overdue payments for over 90 days, is a widely used rule to distinguish between cases in default from non-defaulted ones. Other multi-category schemes could be adopted, but they require a subjective a-priori definition of multiple risk categories, thus adding some bias in the modeling process. To overcome this difficulty, a standard dichotomic setting is used as the basic input for model development. This is the setting that will be assumed throughout the presentation in this chapter. Once an appropriate model is constructed, its output can be mapped to multiple rating classes, as explained in the previous chapter.

M. Doumpos et al., *Analytical Techniques in the Assessment of Credit Risk*, EURO Advanced Tutorials on Operational Research,
https://doi.org/10.1007/978-3-319-99411-6_3

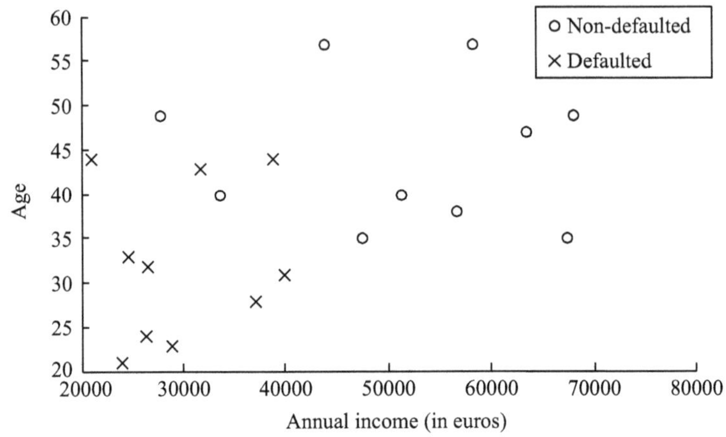

Fig. 3.1 An example of binary classification task for constructing a credit rating model

The construction of a credit scoring/rating model from a sample of m observations involving loans and borrowers in default and non-default, is a learning task. The given sample is referred as training set and is used to infer a decision model $f(\mathbf{x})$ aggregating the input data in the vector $\mathbf{x} = (x_1, x_2, \ldots, x_n)$ for a set of n risk attributes. The model must be constructed such that describes the sample observations as accurately as possible. In an ideal case, the credit model should classify all defaulted cases in the default group and all non-defaulted cases in the non-default class. However, a perfect discrimination is impossible in realistic situations, because there is never enough information to describe defaults in a perfect way; there are always uncontrolled factors that may lead to default.

An illustration of the above classification task is shown in Fig. 3.1. A sample of 20 borrowers derived from the loan portfolio of a credit institution is described in terms of two risk rating attributes: annual income and age. The borrowers in the sample are labeled as "defaulted" (the points marked with crosses) and "non-defaulted" (the points marked with cycles), depending on whether they have been able to meet their obligations and repay their loans according to the agreed terms. Using this basic information, the objective of the analyst is to construct a credit model that is a function of the two risk attributes, f(income, age), such that the model provides as accurate recommendations as possible for the default status of the borrowers. The model should have generalizing ability, meaning that it should lead to good decisions not just for the 20 cases shown in the illustration, but also for other borrowers that will be analyzed through the model in the future. In that sense, the analysis should seek to "learn" a good model from the 20 given examples, which will be applicable (i.e., it can be extrapolated) to other cases, too.

Figure 3.2 shows three different types of decision models for the example data. The first one (upper left graph) is a linear model of the form

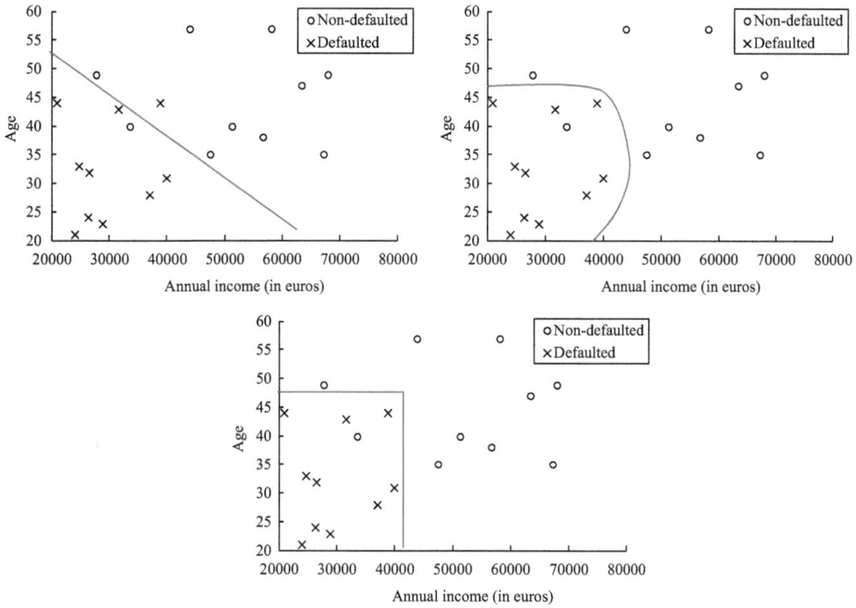

Fig. 3.2 Three types of decision models for the example data

$$f(\text{Income}, \text{Age}) = \alpha + \beta_1(\text{Income}) + \beta_2(\text{Age})$$

where β_1 and β_2 are coefficients that define the slope of the separating line and α defines the location of the line as opposed to the origin.

The upper right graph corresponds to a model in which income and age are combined through a smooth non-linear function. The bottom graph also corresponds to a non-linear separation of the two classes. This model can be represented through a simple decision rule of the following form:

$$\text{If (Income} < t_1) \text{ and (Age} < t_2) \text{ then (Default), else (Non} - \text{default)}$$

where t_1 and t_2 are decision thresholds corresponding to the income and age of the borrowers.

As shown through the above example, once a set of data is given, one must first decide about the type of decision model to use, and then the parameters of the model must be estimated to maximize the discriminating power of the model. The parameter estimation process is referred to as *model fitting* or *model construction*. For example, in the case of the linear model, the constant term α and the coefficients β_1 and β_2 must be estimated. The decision rule model requires the specification of the decision thresholds t_1 and t_2.

Once the parameters of the model are estimated, it can be applied to any new case (borrower) to classify it into one of the predefined classes and estimate the associated PD.

3.2 Modeling Approaches

The model fitting process can be implemented with various methodological approaches, which adopt consider different types of models (from simple linear models up to complex non-linear representations), model fitting criteria, and estimation procedures. In the following sections, we describe the main characteristics for some of the most popular techniques in the field of credit scoring and rating.

3.2.1 *Statistical Models*

3.2.1.1 Naïve Bayes Classifier

The Bayes decision rule sets describes the above classification setting in a very simple probabilistic context. According to Bayes' theorem the conditional probability $\Pr(Y|X)$ of event Y given event X, is given as follows:

$$\Pr(Y|X) = \frac{\Pr(Y)\Pr(X|Y)}{\Pr(X)}$$

As explained earlier, the development of a credit scoring and rating model is based on a binary classification setting, involving two classes. In this context, we can let Y correspond to the status of a borrower ($Y = ND$ for non-defaulted borrowers and $Y = D$ for defaulted ones) and X correspond to the information available on the selected risk rating attributes, i.e., the vector $\mathbf{x} = (x_1, x_2, \ldots, x_n)$. To simplify the notation, we shall use the following conversions (where $k = D$ for the default class and $k = ND$ for non-defaults):

$$\begin{aligned}
\pi_k &\equiv \Pr(Y = k) \\
\Pr(\mathbf{x}) &\equiv \Pr(X = \mathbf{x}) \\
\Pr(k|\mathbf{x}) &\equiv \Pr(Y = k|X=\mathbf{x}) \\
\Pr(\mathbf{x}|k) &\equiv \Pr(X = \mathbf{x}|Y = k)
\end{aligned}$$

Then, we can use Bayes' theorem to model the posterior probability of default (or equivalent the probability of non-default), given the available information about a borrower as expressed through the data vector $\mathbf{x}$:

$$\Pr(D|\mathbf{x}) = \frac{\pi_D \Pr(\mathbf{x}|D)}{\Pr(\mathbf{x})} \tag{3.1}$$

where

- π_D is the a priori probability of default, which is independent of the characteristics of a specific borrower (i.e., it is the same for all borrowers),
- $\Pr(\mathbf{x})$ is the probability of a borrower having the specific attribute vector $\mathbf{x}$,
- $\Pr(\mathbf{x}|D)$ is the conditional probability that a defaulted borrower has the specific attribute vector $\mathbf{x}$.

The a priori probability of default can be specified rather easily through data published frequently by authorities like central banks and national statistical agencies about the default rates at a country level. Usually, it ranges around 5%.

In a binary classification setting, the probability $\Pr(\mathbf{x})$ can be written as follows:

$$\Pr(\mathbf{x}) = \pi_D \Pr(\mathbf{x}|D) + \pi_{ND} \Pr(\mathbf{x}|ND) \tag{3.2}$$

where π_{ND} is the a priori probability of default, i.e., $\pi_{ND} = 1 - \pi_D$.

Substituting (3.2) to (3.1) yields:

$$\Pr(D|\mathbf{x}) = \frac{\pi_D \Pr(\mathbf{x}|D)}{\pi_D \Pr(\mathbf{x}|D) + \pi_{ND} \Pr(\mathbf{x}|ND)} \tag{3.3}$$

To use this expression, we need to estimate the conditional probabilities $\Pr(\mathbf{x}|D)$ and $\Pr(\mathbf{x}|ND)$. Generally, the specification of these probabilities is not a straightforward task. In the naïve Bayes model, it is assumed that the risk attributes $x_1, x_2, \ldots, x_n$ are conditionally independent, which implies that the product rule can be used:

$$\Pr(\mathbf{x}|k) = \prod_{j=1}^{n} \Pr(x_j|k) \tag{3.4}$$

where $\Pr(x_j|k)$ is the probability of having a specific value for attribute j, for borrowers from class k.

Example

Consider the data set of Table 3.1, which consists of 15 non-defaulted firms and 5 defaulted ones, described by three risk attributes:

- net income (profits/losses),
- sales trend (increasing/decreasing),
- credit history (positive for firms with no past defaults, negative for firms with past credit events).

Table 3.1 Example data for naïve Bayes default prediction

Net income (x_1)	Sales trend (x_2)	Credit history (x_3)	Status
Positive	Decreasing	Positive	Non-defaulted
Positive	Increasing	Positive	Non-defaulted
Positive	Increasing	Positive	Non-defaulted
Negative	Increasing	Negative	Non-defaulted
Positive	Increasing	Positive	Non-defaulted
Positive	Decreasing	Negative	Non-defaulted
Negative	Increasing	Positive	Non-defaulted
Positive	Increasing	Positive	Non-defaulted
Negative	Increasing	Positive	Non-defaulted
Negative	Increasing	Positive	Non-defaulted
Negative	Increasing	Positive	Non-defaulted
Positive	Increasing	Negative	Non-defaulted
Negative	Decreasing	Positive	Non-defaulted
Positive	Increasing	Negative	Non-defaulted
Positive	Decreasing	Positive	Non-defaulted
Negative	Decreasing	Negative	Defaulted
Negative	Increasing	Positive	Defaulted
Negative	Increasing	Negative	Defaulted
Negative	Decreasing	Negative	Defaulted
Positive	Increasing	Negative	Defaulted

Based on these data, a credit institution would like to estimate the probability of default for a firm with losses, increasing sales, and positive credit history, if the a priori probability of default is $\pi_D = 0.05$.

The firm under consideration is described by the following "vector":

$$\mathbf{x} = (\text{negative net income, increasing sales, positive history})$$

To calculate the conditional probabilities $\Pr(\mathbf{x}|D)$ and $\Pr(\mathbf{x}|ND)$, the product rule (3.4) will be used. Below we illustrate the process for $\Pr(\mathbf{x}|ND)$:

From the data in Table 3.1, it is evident that 6 out of the 15 non-defaulted firms have losses. Thus, the (empirical) probability that a non-defaulted firm has losses is:

$$\Pr(x_1 = \text{negative}|ND) = \frac{6}{15}$$

Similarly, there are 11 non-defaulted firms with increasing sales, meaning that the probability that a non-defaulted firm has increasing sales is:

$$\Pr(x_2 = \text{increasing sales}|ND) = \frac{11}{15}$$

In the same manner, it can be observed that the probability of a non-defaulted firm having positive credit history is:

$$\Pr(x_3 = \text{positive history}|ND) = \frac{11}{15}$$

Combining these probabilities through the product rule (3.4), yields the probability that a non-defaulted firm has all the above characteristics:

$$\Pr(\mathbf{x}|ND) = \left(\frac{6}{15}\right)\left(\frac{11}{15}\right)\left(\frac{11}{15}\right) = 0.215$$

Following the same approach for the defaulted class, the probability $\Pr(\mathbf{x}|D)$ is found to be equal to 0.1. Substituting to (3.3) and considering that $\pi_{ND} = 1 - \pi_D = 0.95$, gives an estimate for the probability of non-default for the firm under consideration, of $\Pr(D|\mathbf{x}) = 0.024$.

An obvious problem that arises when generalizing this idea to more realistic cases, is that with continuous (quantitative) data rather that the categorical (qualitative) ones used in the above example, the probability calculations cannot be done through simple frequency counts. One option to address this problem, would be to discretize the data, while another possibility would be to assume a specific probability distribution for each attribute (e.g., the normal distribution). Things become more complicated if the conditional independence assumption is dropped, in which case the product rule (3.4) is no longer applicable.

3.2.1.2 Discriminant Analysis

Discriminant analysis extends the naïve Bayes classifier to a more general setting, without considering the conditional independence assumption. More specifically, discriminant analysis assumes that the risk attributes in risk class k ($k \in \{D, ND\}$) are multivariate normally distributed with class average vector $\boldsymbol{\mu}_k = (\mu_{k1}, \mu_{k2}, \ldots, \mu_{kn})$ and covariance matrix $\boldsymbol{\Sigma}_k$. Thus, the conditional probability $\Pr(\mathbf{x}|k)$ has the following density:

$$\Pr(\mathbf{x}|k) = \frac{1}{\sqrt{(2\pi)^n \mid \boldsymbol{\Sigma}_k \mid}} e^{0.5(\mathbf{x}-\boldsymbol{\mu}_k)^\top \boldsymbol{\Sigma}_k^{-1}(\mathbf{x}-\boldsymbol{\mu}_k)} \tag{3.5}$$

where $|\boldsymbol{\Sigma}_k|$ is the determinant of $\boldsymbol{\Sigma}_k$.

From the Bayes formula (3.3) it can be observed that the comparison of the probabilities $\Pr(D|\mathbf{x})$ and $\Pr(ND|\mathbf{x})$ depends only on the nominator, i.e., the conditional probabilities Pr($\mathbf{x}|D$) and Pr($\mathbf{x}|ND$) as well as the prior probabilities π_D and π_{ND}. Thus, the decision rule can be expressed as follows: a borrower is classified in the default class if

$$\pi_D \Pr(\mathbf{x}|D) > \pi_{ND} \Pr(\mathbf{x}|ND) \tag{3.6}$$

The two sides of this inequality can be described through a pair of discriminant functions $f_D(\mathbf{x})$ and $f_{ND}(\mathbf{x})$, defined as follows:

$$\begin{aligned} f_k(x) &= \log[\pi_k \Pr(\mathbf{x}|k)] \\ &= \log\pi_k - \frac{1}{2}\log\mid \boldsymbol{\Sigma}_k \mid - \frac{1}{2}\boldsymbol{\mu}_k^\top \boldsymbol{\Sigma}_k^{-1}\boldsymbol{\mu}_k + \mathbf{x}^\top \boldsymbol{\Sigma}_k^{-1}\boldsymbol{\mu}_k - \frac{1}{2}\mathbf{x}^\top \boldsymbol{\Sigma}_k^{-1}\mathbf{x} \end{aligned}$$

This is a quadratic function of the form

$$f_k(\mathbf{x}) = \alpha_k + \sum_{j=1}^{n} \beta_{kj} x_j + \sum_{i,j=1}^{n} \gamma_{kij} x_i x_j$$

where the constant term α_k, the coefficients vector $\boldsymbol{\beta}_k = (\beta_{k1}, \ldots, \beta_{kn})$, and the matrix $\boldsymbol{\Gamma}_k = (\gamma_{kij})$ of the quadratic terms are given by:

$$\begin{aligned} \alpha_k &= \log\pi_k - \frac{1}{2}\log|\boldsymbol{\Sigma}_k| - \frac{1}{2}\boldsymbol{\mu}_k^\top \boldsymbol{\Sigma}_k^{-1}\boldsymbol{\mu}_k \\ \boldsymbol{\beta}_k &= \boldsymbol{\Sigma}_k^{-1}\boldsymbol{\mu}_k \\ \boldsymbol{\Gamma}_k &= -\frac{1}{2}\boldsymbol{\Sigma}_k^{-1} \end{aligned}$$

It is worth noting that if it is assumed that the covariance matrices $\boldsymbol{\Sigma}_D$ and $\boldsymbol{\Sigma}_{ND}$ do not have statistically significant differences, then they can be replaced by a common covariance matrix $\boldsymbol{\Sigma}$. In this case, the quadratic part and the term $\frac{1}{2}\log\mid \boldsymbol{\Sigma}_k \mid$, are the same for both discriminant functions. Thus, they can be omitted, leading to linear discriminant functions:

$$f_k(\mathbf{x}) = \alpha_k + \sum_{j=1}^{n} \beta_{kj} x_j$$

with

$$\alpha_k = \log\pi_k - \frac{1}{2}\boldsymbol{\mu}_k^\top \boldsymbol{\Sigma}^{-1}\boldsymbol{\mu}_k$$

$$\boldsymbol{\beta}_k = \boldsymbol{\Sigma}^{-1}\boldsymbol{\mu}_k$$

Moreover, the decision rule (3.6) can be simplified further leading to a single classification function, instead of the two discriminant functions described above. More specifically, taking the logarithm of (3.6), a borrower is classified in the default class if the following inequality holds:

$$\log\frac{\pi_{ND}}{\pi_D} + \log\frac{\Pr(\mathbf{x}|ND)}{\Pr(\mathbf{x}|D)} < 0$$

Substituting (3.5) to this inequality and assuming a common covariance matrix $\boldsymbol{\Sigma}$, yields the following (linear) decision rule: a borrower is assigned to the default class if the following inequality holds:

$$\log\frac{\pi_{ND}}{\pi_D} - \frac{1}{2}(\boldsymbol{\mu}_D + \boldsymbol{\mu}_{ND})^\top \boldsymbol{\Sigma}^{-1}(\boldsymbol{\mu}_{ND} - \boldsymbol{\mu}_D) + \mathbf{x}^\top \boldsymbol{\Sigma}^{-1}(\boldsymbol{\mu}_{ND} - \boldsymbol{\mu}_D) < 0$$

The main advantage of linear discriminant analysis over the quadratic form is that the latter is more sensitive to the statistical properties of the data, as more and higher quality data are needed to estimate accurately the class covariance matrices.

Under the underlying assumptions noted above (i.e., multivariate normality and known class covariance matrices), discriminant analysis yields the optimal classification rule (in linear or quadratic form). However, such assumptions are quite strict, and they typically do not hold in most practical cases for credit scoring and rating data.

3.2.1.3 Logistic Regression

Logistic regression (LR) is probably the most widely used method for developing credit scoring and rating models. It is also widely used in many other areas in finance and business, in general.

Similarly to linear discriminant analysis, LR is based on a linear decision rule. More specifically, using the non-default class as the reference category, LR assumes that the log of odds ratio is a linear function of the risk attributes:

$$\log\frac{\Pr(ND|\mathbf{x})}{\Pr(D|\mathbf{x})} = \alpha + \beta_1 x_1 + \cdots + \beta_n x_n$$

Given that $\Pr(D|\mathbf{x}) = 1 - \Pr(ND|\mathbf{x})$, it is easy to see that the probability of non-default can be derived from the above log of odds ratio as follows:

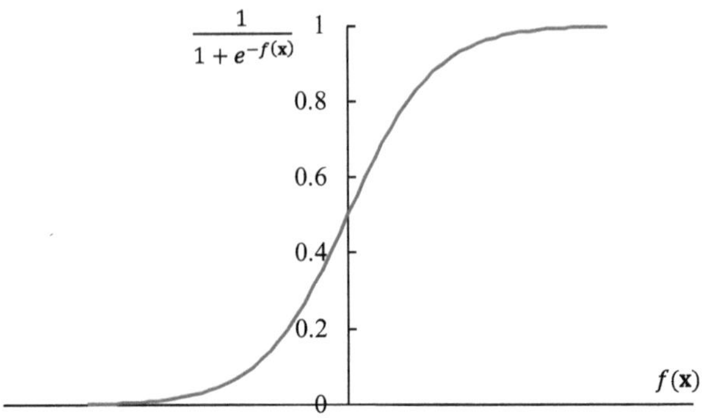

Fig. 3.3 Form of the logistic function

$$\Pr(ND|\mathbf{x}) = \frac{1}{1+e^{-f(\mathbf{x})}} \tag{3.7}$$

where $f(\mathbf{x}) = \alpha + \beta_1 x_1 + \cdots + \beta_n x_n$. The above expression is known as the logistic function. It defines a non-linear (logistic) mapping of the log of odds function $f(\mathbf{x})$ to a probability scale. Naturally, it is bounded between 0 and 1, as shown in Fig. 3.3, and it is equal to 0.5, if $f(\mathbf{x}) = 0$. A straightforward decision rule is to assign a borrower to the non-default class if $\Pr(ND|\mathbf{x}) > 0.5$, which is equivalent to $f(\mathbf{x}) > 0$.

The estimation of the parameters of the logistic model (3.7) can be done with standard numerical optimization techniques. Instead of relying on the normality assumptions of discriminant analysis, which lead to closed-form solutions, LR adopts a more general framework based on maximum likelihood estimation. Given a training data set of m borrowers, including borrowers in default ($y = 0$) and non-defaulted cases ($y = 1$), the objective is to find the best estimates for the constant term α and the coefficients vector $\boldsymbol{\beta}$, such that the probabilities derived with (3.7) are as close as possible to 1 for the non-defaulted cases and close to 0 for the defaulted cases. This is expressed through the following likelihood function:

$$L(\alpha, \boldsymbol{\beta}) = \prod_{i=1}^{m} \Pr(1|\mathbf{x}_i)^{y_i}[1 - \Pr(1|\mathbf{x}_i)]^{1-y_i}$$

Substituting (3.7) for $\Pr(1|\mathbf{x}_i)$ and taking the logarithm, yields the log-likelihood function:

$$\mathcal{L}(\alpha, \boldsymbol{\beta}) = \sum_{i=1}^{m} \left[y_i f(\mathbf{x}_i) - \ln\left(1 + e^{f(\mathbf{x}_i)}\right)\right] \tag{3.8}$$

This is convex function of $n + 1$ variables (the constant term α and the coefficients $\beta_1, \ldots, \beta_n$), which can be maximized by taking the derivatives and setting them equal to 0. This leads to a system of non-linear equations, which can be solved easily with iterative algorithms (e.g., Newton-Raphson).

Although the above process does not yield a closed-form solution, maximum likelihood techniques are widely used in statistical estimation and inference. One of the benefits of the estimation process, is that the results for the parameters (constant term and coefficients) are accompanied by hypothesis tests about their significance, thus allowing the analyst to identify important variables that contribute to the analysis.

3.2.2 *Machine Learning*

A common characteristic of statistical techniques, such as the ones described in the previous subsections, is that the decision model is pre-assumed to be linear or quadratic. This is a convenient approach, because it simplifies the modeling process. However, it can be restrictive in a general setting, when credit scoring and rating cannot be modeled accurately through simple decision models. Machine learning techniques adopt data-driven schemes allowing the derivation of more general and flexible models from data, without making statistical assumptions. There is a wide variety of machine learning approaches that have been used for credit risk analysis. Below, we describe three popular schemes, namely decision tree models, neural networks, and ensembles.

3.2.2.1 Classification Trees

Symbolic models are widely used for data classification. Such models have two very similar forms: decision rules and classification trees. Decision rules are expressed in if-then form, with the conditions' part defining a conjunction of elementary conditions on the risk rating attributes and the conclusion part providing a recommendation about the expected status of a borrower (default/non-default) when all conditions are satisfied. Classification trees provide a convenient way to represent decision rules, in the form of a dichotomic tree structure.

An example of a classification tree is presented in Fig. 3.4. As shown in this illustration, a classification tree is a hierarchical structure consisting of multiple elementary dichotomic splits. Each split is defined by a risk attribute (x) and a cut-off value (t), thus corresponding to an if-then-else decision rule of the form "If $x \geq t$ then …, else …". The top node (root) of the tree corresponds to the most general split that applies to all cases, whereas nodes at lower levels of the hierarchy involve more special cases. Every series of consecutive splits leads to one leaf node (decision node) with a recommendation for borrowers meeting all conditions defined by the splits. In Fig. 3.4 the leaf nodes are represented by circles (D for borrowers that are likely to default and ND for the creditworthy borrowers in the non-default class). For instance, according to the illustrative example a low-income borrower (income < 30,000 €) with loan to value ratio higher than 100% is considered as a high-risk case and is assigned to the default class. Except for providing a

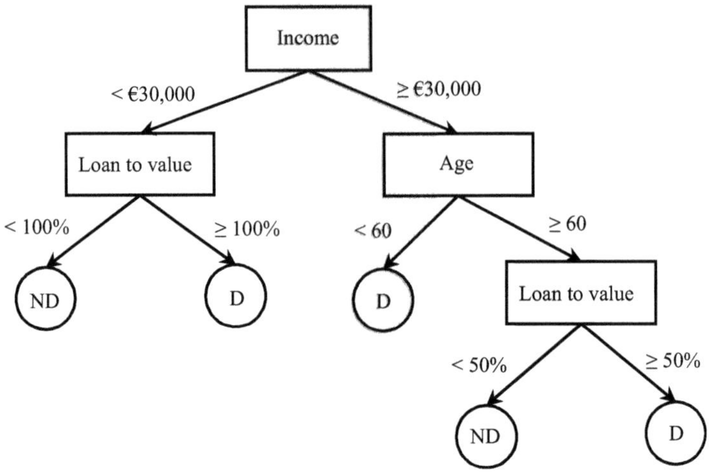

Fig. 3.4 An example of a classification tree

recommendation, the leaf nodes can also be associated with some estimate of the posterior class membership probability (i.e., the probabilities of default and non-default).

The development of a classification tree is performed through an iterative process, starting from the root node. Every stage (node) of this process consists of three individual steps:

1. Evaluation of the discriminating power of the risk attributes using the training cases falling at the node under consideration.
2. Selection of the most discriminating attribute.
3. Specification of the splitting rule for the selected attribute, which provides the best classification.

This procedure is repeated until a termination criterion is met. At a second phase, a pruning process is often performed, which cuts down parts of the tree, which are too specialized and may lead to poor generalizing performance. This leads to a simpler and more general tree, which is easier to understand and implement.

The above process for tree construction can be implemented with different algorithms. Some typical and well-known examples of such algorithms are C4.5 (and its improved version C5.0) as well as CART (classification and regression trees).

Classification trees and decision rules offer a very convenient and nature modeling form for credit risk assessment, and they are computationally applicable to large data sets. Moreover, they can handle qualitative and even missing data in a straightforward manner, without requiring complex data transformations. However, they are often prone to overfitting and their probabilistic outputs do not have a continuous form, as each leaf node is usually associated with only one estimate.

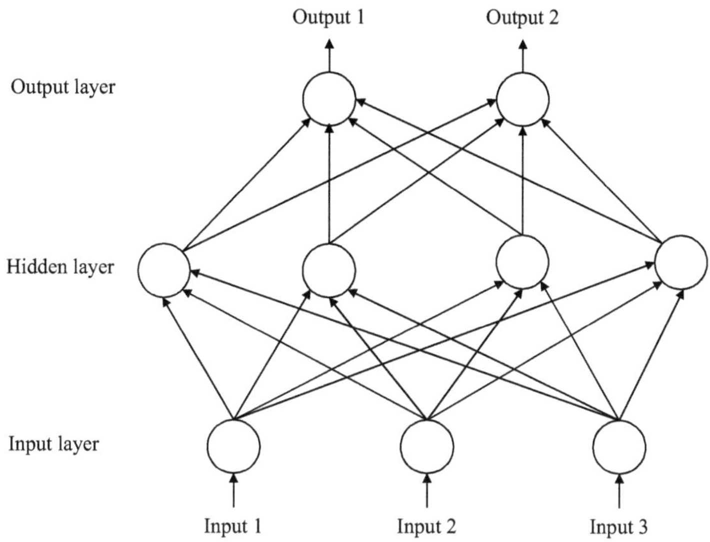

Fig. 3.5 Architecture of a feed-forward NN for a binary classification task

3.2.2.2 Neural Networks

Neural networks (NNs) are a general framework for descriptive and predictive modeling in data intensive tasks. Since the introduction of the perceptron by Frank Rosenblatt in the 1950s, NNs have been at the core of artificial intelligence research, data mining, and machine learning, for modeling complex systems.

A NN is a complex structure of parallel processing units (neurons) organized into different layers. The structure of a NN can be specified in various topologies, each corresponding to different type of a NN model. In this presentation, we shall briefly describe the architecture and operation of multi-layer feedforward NNs. A typical structure of such this type of NN (Fig. 3.5) includes the following structural elements:

1. An input layer consisting of the input risk attributes.
2. An output layer consisting of one or more nodes depending on the form of the desired output of the network. In classification problems, the number of nodes of the output layer is determined depending on the number of groups. A two-group classification problem that is typically considered for constructing in credit risk models, can be modeled using a single output node. In this setting, if the output exceeds a threshold, then the borrower is assigned to the non-default class, otherwise default is more likely. For multi-group problems, the number of outputs is equal to the number of risk classes, in which case the output nodes act in a competitive manner (i.e., the network's output is the class for which the corresponding node yields the maximum output).

3. A series of intermediate layers, referred to as hidden layers. The nodes of each hidden layer are fully connected with nodes in other layers (usually the layers at the preceding and subsequent levels of the hierarchy). There is no general rule to define the number of hidden layers or the number of nodes at these layers. This is usually performed through trial and error processes. Alternatively, algorithmic approaches can also be used to select the optimal structure, at the expense of much higher computational cost.

Each connection between two nodes of the network is assigned a weight representing the strength of the connection. Based on the connections' weights, the input to each node is determined as the weighted average of the outputs of all other nodes with which there is an established connection. Assuming the feedforward structure of Fig. 3.5, where only nodes in consecutive layers are connected, the input I_{ik} to node i of layer k is defined as follows:

$$I_{ik} = \alpha_{ik} + \sum_{j=1}^{d_{k-1}} w_{ji}^{k-1} O_{jk-1}$$

where:

- α_{ik} is a constant (bias) term for node i at layer k,
- d_{k-1} is the number of nodes at layer $k-1$,
- w_{ji}^{k-1} is the weight of the connection from node j at layer $k-1$ to node i at layer k,
- O_{jk-1} is the output of node j at layer $k-1$.

The output of each node is specified through a transformation function. The most common form of this function is the logistic function, which maps the input to an output ranging in [0, 1], as follows:

$$O_{ik} = \frac{1}{1 + e^{-I_{ik}}}$$

The determination of the connections' weights and nodes' biases (training of the network) is accomplished through optimization techniques. The objective of the optimization process is to minimize the differences between the recommendations of the network and the actual classification of the alternatives belonging in the training sample.

The most widely used network training methodology is the back-propagation algorithm, which is a gradient descent algorithm, involving an iterative forward and backward processing of the NN, so that a loss function is minimized. The loss function measures the differences between the output of the network and the actual status of the borrowers in the training set. For classification problems, a typical loss function is the cross-entropy function:

$$C = -\sum_{i=1}^{m} [y_i \ln O_i + (1 - y_i) \ln (1 - O_i)]$$

where O_i is the output of the network for borrower i and $y_i \in \{0, 1\}$ is the known status of the borrower from the training set ($y = 0$ for cases in default and $y = 1$ for non-defaulted ones). If the output node of the network is defined through the logistic function, thus this loss function is actually the same (but with reversed sign) as the log likelihood function (3.8).

However, in the general case, the complex structure of the NN leads to a non-convex loss minimization problem. Back-propagation starts with a random initialization of the NN (weights and biases), calculates the error for the training data, and then back-propagates the error by updating the weights and the biases, so that the error is reduced. This is done iteratively, until a convergence/stopping criterion is met.

The major advantage of neural networks is their parallel processing ability as well as their ability to represent highly complex data. Theoretically, this enables the approximation of any real function with infinite accuracy. The general nature and strong analytical/predictive power of NNs, that made them a very popular tool with wide-spread applications in many areas in finance and business, including credit risk modeling. On the other hand, the criticism on the use of NNs has been main focused on their inability to provide explanations of the network's results. This is a significant shortcoming, mainly from a decision support perspective, since credit analysts should be able to support and explain the structure of the model used to derive risk estimates. Nevertheless, it should be noted that this shortcoming is also relevant for many machine learning models, which are based on general and complex modeling architectures. Moreover, several new types of NN architectures and learning schemes have been developed (e.g., convolutional NNs), which have gained widespread interest due to their superior predictive performance in large-scale problems and deep leaning systems.

3.2.2.3 Ensembles

Ensembles refer to complex modeling approaches based on the combination of multiple decision models developed by one or more learning algorithms. Using a combination of different models may lead to improved results, by reducing the bias and/or the variance of the outputs of individual models. The bias-variance trade-off is a well-known issue when inferring decision models from data. Given a data-driven scheme for model construction, such as the one used for credit scoring and rating models, the expected performance (error or accuracy rate) of a model depends on the training data used for model fitting. The data incorporate noise, they are incomplete, and may be subject to several statistical limitations (e.g., outliers, high correlations, etc.). Thus, the expected performance of a model fitting approach, depends on the bias of the derived model and its variability. Bias is reduced by making weaker modeling assumptions (e.g., discriminant analysis and logistic regression have high bias because they assume a specific model structure, whereas NNs and tree model have low bias). However, more flexible models that are based on weaker assumptions, exhibit higher sensitivity to the training data (i.e., higher variance). Ensembles are algorithmic, data-driven procedures, that seek to reduce bias and/or variance through a combination of multiple models.

The idea why model combination might work can be easily understood if one considers a pool of p models with error rates (assuming a 0-1 error scale) of ε_1, ε_2, ..., $\varepsilon_p < 0.5$. If the models provide independent outputs, then the error rate of their combination is simply the product $\varepsilon_1\varepsilon_2\cdots\varepsilon_p$, which will converge to zero as p increases. Of course, the independence assumption is too strong, and it is impossible to derive fully independent models from a data set. Ensembles seek to impose independence by constructing different models from perturbations of the training set. This works best with unstable models, that is models whose outputs are sensitive to the data used during the model fitting process.

Two popular ensemble schemes are bagging and boosting. Bagging stands for bootstrap aggregating and it is a variance reduction technique. Given a training set of m borrowers, bagging starts by constructing B bootstrap samples, each consisting of m cases selected at random (with replacement) from the original dataset. Using a selected learning algorithm (e.g., any of the methods described in this chapter or other similar techniques), B decision models $f_1(\mathbf{x})$, $f_2(\mathbf{x})$, ..., $f_B(\mathbf{x})$ are constructed from each one of the bootstrap samples. The predictions (class outputs) from these models are then combined through a simple majority voting and the result is the most frequent recommendation (default/non-default) among all models.

Boosting follows a different scheme based on an iterative process that yields a sequence of base models $f_1(\mathbf{x})$, $f_2(\mathbf{x})$, ..., all derived from the same data set. Each base model ℓ uses the outputs of the preceding model $\ell - 1$ in the sequence, to define weights for the training instances (borrowers), such that harder instances (i.e., those more difficult to classify correctly) are weighted more than easier ones. Thus, as the iterative process proceeds, more emphasis is put on those cases that matter most, whereas obvious cases gradually become irrelevant. At the end of the process, the combined output is derived by weighting all base models by their predictive performance. In contrast to bagging, boosting decreases both the bias and the variance components of the error rate, but it may be more sensitive to noisy data and outliers.

3.2.3 *Optimization Approaches*

All methods and techniques described earlier employ some form of algorithmic optimization steps for fitting a credit risk/rating model to a set of training data. However, in this subsection we describe separately some approaches that are explicitly based on traditional optimization tools that are very common to the field of operations research, namely mathematical programming models.

The first uses of mathematical programming to construct classification models can be traced back to the 1960s. In a very simple setting a binary classification problem for constructing a linear credit scoring model can be formulated as the following linear program (LP):

$$\begin{array}{lll} \min & \sigma_1 + \sigma_2 + \cdots + \sigma_m & \\ \text{subject to}: & \alpha + \mathbf{x}_i^\top \boldsymbol{\beta} \geq 1 - \sigma_i & \text{for non-defaulted borrowers} \\ & \alpha + \mathbf{x}_i^\top \boldsymbol{\beta} \leq -1 + \sigma_i & \text{for defaulted borrowers} \\ & \alpha, \boldsymbol{\beta} \in \mathbb{R}, \sigma_i \geq 0 & \end{array} \tag{3.9}$$

This LP has m constraints, one for each case in the training data. The first set of constraints apply to non-defaulted cases, whereas the second involves defaulted cases. Similarly to discriminant analysis and logistic regression, a straightforward decision rule for a linear prediction model of the form $f(\mathbf{x}) = \alpha + \mathbf{x}^\top \boldsymbol{\beta}$, is to classify a borrower i to the non-default class if $\alpha + \mathbf{x}_i^\top \boldsymbol{\beta} > 0$ and to the default group if $\alpha + \mathbf{x}_i^\top \boldsymbol{\beta} < 0$. The two constraints transform these strict inequalities to canonical form (greater/lower than or equal to) by adding/subtracting a constant from the right-hand side. Without loss of generality, this constant is set equal to 1 in the above LP formulation. The deviation variables $\sigma_1, \ldots, \sigma_m$ represent the errors for the training data. These errors are defined as follows:

- For non-defaulted borrowers: $\sigma_i = \max\{0, 1 - (\alpha + \mathbf{x}_i^\top \boldsymbol{\beta})\}$
- For defaulted borrowers: $\sigma_i = \max\{0, (\alpha + \mathbf{x}_i^\top \boldsymbol{\beta}) + 1\}$

The objective of the model is to minimize the sum of these errors. However, instead of the sum, mathematical programming formulations enable the use of many other error functions. A commonly used alternative is the total weighted error. In this case, weights are introduced for each class of borrowers, considering the number of borrowers in each risk category as well as misclassification costs (if available). In the simplest case, a common weight $1/m_0$ can be applied to all borrowers from the default class in the training sample, where m_0 is the number of these borrowers. Similarly, a weight of $1/m_1$ is used for the non-defaulted borrowers. This simple weighting scheme overcomes estimation problems that may arise due to the considerable imbalance of defaulted and non-defaulted cases, as the number of defaulted borrowers is usually much smaller than the non-defaulted ones. Thus, the objective function of the above linear program is restated as follows:

$$\min \frac{1}{m_0} \sum_{i \in 0} \sigma_i + \frac{1}{m_1} \sum_{i \in 1} \sigma_i \tag{3.10}$$

The underlying idea of the above LP formulation is illustrated in Fig. 3.6 for a two-dimensional problem ($n = 2$). The linear decision function $f(\mathbf{x})$ defines a separating line (hyperplane when $n > 2$) that distinguishes between defaulted and

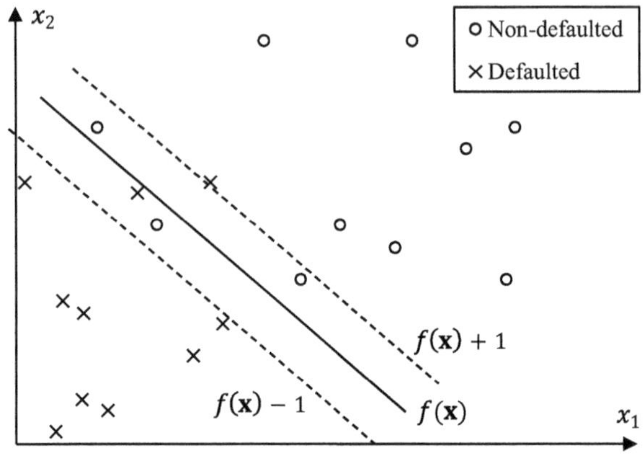

Fig. 3.6 A linear classification task and decision boundaries

non-defaulted borrowers. The two parallels $f(\mathbf{x}) \pm 1$ define a "zone of uncertainty" around the separating line. Non-defaulted borrowers that fall below the line defined by $f(\mathbf{x}) = 1$ have $\sigma > 0$. All other non-defaulted borrowers (i.e., in the area above $f(\mathbf{x}) = 1$), have $\sigma = 0$. Similarly, defaulted borrowers in the area above the line $f(\mathbf{x}) = -1$, also have $\sigma > 0$, whereas defaulted borrowers below this boundary have $\sigma = 0$. In both cases, the error variables represent the deviations (violations) from the two boundaries. Minimizing the sum of these errors is a proxy for minimizing the number of violations of the decision boundary.

The above simple idea can be extended in many ways through more elaborate mathematical programming formulations, linear and non-linear. The most well-known approach based on this framework is support vector machines (SVMs). SVMs combine statistical learning principles with mathematical optimization into a comprehensive well-founded framework.

SVMs implement the idea of Tikhonov's regularization, which describes ill-posed systems of linear equations of the form $\mathbf{Ax} = \mathbf{b}$, that may not have a solution and the inverse of matrix $\mathbf{A}$ may exhibit instabilities (i.e., $\mathbf{A}$ may be singular or ill-conditioned). In such cases, a numerically robust solution $\mathbf{x}$ can be obtained by minimizing $||\mathbf{Ax} - \mathbf{b}||^2 + \lambda||\mathbf{x}||^2$, where $\lambda > 0$ is a regularization parameter that defines the trade-off between the error term $||\mathbf{Ax} - \mathbf{b}||^2$ and the "size" of the solution (thus controlling the solution for changes in $\mathbf{A}$ and $\mathbf{b}$).

Adapting this framework to the binary classification task described above, the squared error $||\mathbf{Ax} - \mathbf{b}||^2$ can be replaced by the sum of absolute errors $\sigma_1 + \sigma_2 + \cdots + \sigma_m$, whereas the regularization term is defined by $||\boldsymbol{\beta}||^2$. It is worth noting that the separating margin between the two hyperplanes $f(\mathbf{x}) = \pm 1$ is equal to $2/||\boldsymbol{\beta}||$. Thus, the regularization principle can be described in geometric terms, as the search for a decision rule that minimizes classification error, while maximizing the separating margin between the classes. Moreover, it can be shown that there exists a theoretical upper bound on the expected classification error, which is defined by the error of a model for the training data (empirical risk) and an uncertainty term, that involves among others, the abovementioned separating margin.

Under this setting the previous LP formulation can be re-expressed into the following quadratic programming (QP) form:

$$\begin{array}{lll} \min & \frac{1}{2}\|\boldsymbol{\beta}\|^2 + \lambda \sum_{i=1}^{m} \sigma_i & \\ \text{subject to :} & \alpha + \mathbf{x}_i^\top \boldsymbol{\beta} \geq 1 - \sigma_i & \text{for non-defaulted borrowers} \\ & \alpha + \mathbf{x}_i^\top \boldsymbol{\beta} \leq -1 + \sigma_i & \text{for defaulted borrowers} \\ & \alpha, \boldsymbol{\beta} \in \mathbb{R}, \sigma_i \geq 0 & \end{array}$$

Even though this is not an LP anymore, it can be solved very efficiently for large data sets with different existing mathematical programming solvers, given that it is a typical convex optimization problem (QP). This is the standard context for linear SVM models.

The same principles can also be extended to non-linear decision models. To this end, it is helpful to consider the Lagrangian dual of the above QP problem. To facilitate the presentation, we follow the standard notation in the SVM literature, assuming that the two classes of borrowers are denoted by $y = 1$ (non-default) and $y = -1$ (defaults), rather than the 0/1 notation used up to this point. Thus, the previous QP problem can be re-stated as follows:

$$\begin{array}{lll} \min & \frac{1}{2}\|\boldsymbol{\beta}\|^2 + \lambda \sum_{i=1}^{m} \sigma_i & \\ \text{subject to :} & y_i\left(\alpha + \mathbf{x}_i^\top \boldsymbol{\beta}\right) \geq 1 - \sigma_i & \forall i = 1, \ldots, m \\ & \alpha, \boldsymbol{\beta} \in \mathbb{R}, \sigma_i \geq 0 & \end{array}$$

Denoting by $u_1, u_2, \ldots, u_m$ the dual variables associated with the constraints, the Lagrangian dual is:

$$\begin{array}{lll} \max & \sum_{i=1}^{m} u_i - \frac{1}{2} \sum_{i,j=1}^{m} u_i u_j y_i y_j \mathbf{x}_i^\top \mathbf{x}_i & \\ \text{subject to :} & \sum_{i=1}^{m} y_i u_i = 0 & \\ & 0 \leq u_i \leq \lambda & \forall i = 1, \ldots, m \end{array}$$

The solution of the dual is such that $u_i > 0$ only for borrowers for which the inequality $y_i\left(\alpha + \mathbf{x}_i^\top \boldsymbol{\beta}\right) \geq 1 - \sigma_i$ is active at the primal problem. These cases represent the support vectors, i.e., the data observations that define the model.

Using the standard Karush-Kuhn-Tucker optimality conditions, it can be shown that the optimal coefficients vector $\boldsymbol{\beta}$ is expressed in terms of the dual solution as follows:

$$\boldsymbol{\beta} = \sum_{i=1}^{m} u_i y_i \mathbf{x}_i$$

This implies that the optimal decision function $f(\mathbf{x}) = \alpha + \mathbf{x}^\top \boldsymbol{\beta}$, can be stated in the following form:

$$f(\mathbf{x}) = \alpha + \sum_{i=1}^{m} u_i y_i \mathbf{x}^\top \mathbf{x}_i$$

Thus, if the linear model $(\mathbf{x}) = \alpha + \mathbf{x}^\top \boldsymbol{\beta}$ is replaced by a non-linear form $f(\mathbf{x}) = \alpha + \mathbf{g}(\mathbf{x})^\top \boldsymbol{\beta}$, where $\mathbf{g}(\mathbf{x}) = [g_1(\mathbf{x}), g_2(\mathbf{x}), \ldots]$ is an arbitrary mapping of the n input risk attributes to a higher dimensional feature space, then the above expression still applies, by replacing the (linear) inner products $\mathbf{x}^\top \mathbf{x}_i$ with $\mathbf{g}(\mathbf{x})^\top \mathbf{g}(\mathbf{x}_i)$. The non-linear mapping **g** does not have to be specified explicitly. Instead, it is defined implicitly through a kernel function K, such that $K(\mathbf{x}, \mathbf{x}') = \mathbf{g}(\mathbf{x})^\top \mathbf{g}(\mathbf{x}')$. Thus, the decision model is expressed as follows:

$$f(\mathbf{x}) = \alpha + \sum_{i=1}^{m} u_i y_i K(\mathbf{x}, \mathbf{x}')$$

For instance, the quadratic kernel $K(\mathbf{x}, \mathbf{x}') = (1 + \mathbf{x}^\top \mathbf{x}')$ transforms the n-dimensional input data to a higher dimensional space defined by attributes $\left(1, x_1, x_2, \ldots, x_n, x_1^2, x_2^2, \ldots, x_n^2, x_1 x_2, \ldots\right)$. Mapping the data through the kernel function to a higher dimensional feature space, enables the application of the ideas of linear separation to a much more complex structure of the data.

3.2.4 Multicriteria Decision Aiding

From the methodological point of view, credit scoring for business and consumer loans is a statistical pattern classification problem, as the decision models are constructed based on historical default data.[1] Nevertheless, some features that analysts often require scoring models to have, make decision analysis techniques, and multicriteria decision aiding (MCDA), in particular, quite appealing in this context. More specifically:

- Credit scoring models are usually required to be monotone with respect to the inputs. From an economic and business perspective, the monotonicity assumption implies that as the input information for a given applicant improves, the estimated

[1] In other specialized credit granting contexts (e.g., project finance), the risk assessment process is mostly based on empirical quantitative and qualitative models.

probability of default should decrease. Assuming that all attributes are in a maximization form, monotonicity implies that $\Pr(D|\mathbf{x}_i) \leq \Pr(D|\mathbf{x}_j)$, for all borrowers i and j such that $x_{ik} \geq x_{jk}$ for all risk attributes $k = 1, \ldots, n$. Models that violate monotonicity in an arbitrary manner may fail to be accepted, because they lack economic sense, thus providing counterintuitive results from an economic perspective. Furthermore, empirical results have shown that introducing monotonicity in credit scoring models often improves their predictive performance and robustness, through the elimination of the over-fitting effect.
- Credit scoring models should be transparent and comprehensible. The predictive accuracy of credit scoring models is not the sole decisive factor for their success in practice. In addition to being accurate, the modes should also be easy to understand by analysts, end users, and regulators. A comprehensible model enables its user to understand its underlying logic and provide justifications on its recommendations, instead of simply being used as a black-box analytic recommendation tool.
- Risk grades are ordinal. This is often ignored by many popular statistical and computational intelligence techniques used for model building, which often assume that the classes are nominal (i.e., in no order).

Multicriteria decision models fit well these requirements: (a) they are ordinal and provide evaluation results that are monotone with respect to the evaluation criteria, and (b) they promote transparency, enabling the credit analyst to calibrate them based on his/her expert domain knowledge, allowing for justification of the obtained results. Among others, MCDA methods have been used in credit scoring (and the relevant field of bankruptcy prediction) in different ways, such as:

- Building accurate and transparent credit scoring systems, customized to the needs of financial institutions, enhancing judgmental approaches.
- In combination with other modeling and learning techniques, including methods such as the ones described above.
- As optimization approaches for model fitting under multiple performance measures (e.g., using multi-objective optimizers).
- As alternatives to existing statistical and machine learning approaches.

Multicriteria decision models are expressed in various functional, relational, and symbolic (rule-based) forms. Below we outline two types of multicriteria models, namely value function models and outranking models.

3.2.4.1 Value Function Models

Value function models in MCDA originate from utility theory, which is a fundamental tool in decision analysis. In a multicriteria context, multiattribute utility/value theory (MAUT/MAVT) provides a normative approach for decision making in problems involving a finite set of alternatives (i.e., choices) described by multiple decision criteria. In the context of credit risk assessment, the alternatives are the borrowers/loans and the criteria refer to the risk attributes that are used to assess their creditworthiness.

MAVT is involved with functional decision models (value functions) aggregating multiple criteria into a composite indicator. A value function V aggregates a vector $\mathbf{x}$ of n decision criteria such that:

$$V(\mathbf{x}_i) > V(\mathbf{x}_j) \Rightarrow \text{alternative } i \text{ is preferred over alternative } j \ (\mathbf{x}_i \succ \mathbf{x}_j)$$
$$V(\mathbf{x}_i) = V(\mathbf{x}_j) \Rightarrow \text{alternatives } i \text{ and } j \text{ are indifferent } (\mathbf{x}_i \sim \mathbf{x}_j)$$

In the context of credit risk assessment, the global value $V(\mathbf{x})$ provides an estimate of the overall creditworthiness and default risk of the borrowers, in a predefined scale (usually between 0 and 1). Thus, the above conditions imply that if the credit score of borrower i is higher than that of another borrower j, then the former is more creditworthy than the latter, whereas if the credit scores are the same then both borrowers have the same level of credit risk.

Depending on the criteria independence conditions, different form of value functions can be defined. For instance, under the mutual preferential independence condition, an additive value function (AVF) can be assumed:

$$V(\mathbf{x}) = \sum_{k=1}^{n} w_k v_k(x_k)$$

In this case, the overall credit score of a borrower is a weighted average of partial scores, defined by the marginal value functions $v_1(x_1), \ldots, v_n(x_n)$ for the risk assessment criteria. Without loss of generality, it can be assumed that the weighting constants are non-negative and normalized such that $w_1 + w_2 + \ldots + w_n = 1$. The marginal value functions, which define the partial scores, are scaled such that $v_k(x_{k*}) = 0$ and $v_k(x_k^*) = 1$, where x_{k*} and x_k^* are the most and least risky level of risk attribute k, respectively. For simplicity, henceforth it will be assumed that all risk assessment criteria are expressed in maximization form (thus implying that all marginal value functions are non-decreasing). This additive model can be linear or nonlinear depending on the form of the marginal value functions.

Under weaker preferential independence assumptions alternative value models can be introduced. For instance, a multiplicative value functions expressed as follows:

$$V(\mathbf{x}) = \prod_{k=1}^{n} [1 + \lambda w_k v_k(x_k)]$$

where $\lambda > -1$ is a scaling constant, such that $1 + \lambda = \prod_{k=1}^{n} [1 + \lambda w_k]$. In the case $\lambda = 0$, the multiplicative function reduces to an additive one.

Under the more general setting, the multilinear value function can be considered:

$$V(\mathbf{x}) = \sum_{k=1}^{n} w_k v_k(x_k) + \sum_{k=1}^{n} \sum_{\ell>k} w_{k\ell} v_k(x_k) v_\ell(x_\ell) + \sum_{k=1}^{n} \sum_{\ell>k}$$
$$\times \sum_{z>\ell} w_{k\ell z} v_k(x_k) v_\ell(x_\ell) v_z(x_z) + w_{123\ldots} \prod_{k=1}^{n} v_k(x_k)$$

This general model has $2^n - 1$ scaling constants as opposed to n trade-offs involved in the additive and multiplicative forms and includes these two simpler models as special cases. However, the additional complexity of the multilinear model makes it difficult to use in cases with $n \geq 4$.

For the remainder we shall focus on AVFs, which retain the simplicity and comprehensibility of linear models, but it is a more general type of model, because it allows for some non-linearity. Additive models are extensively used for credit risk modeling and scoring/rating, because they are intuitive, simple to understand and implement, and they are compatible with the scorecard structure of many credit rating systems used in practice.

The construction of the additive credit evaluation model can be simplified by replacing the products $w_k v_k(x_k)$, $k = 1, \ldots, n$, with a set of rescaled marginal value functions $u_1, \ldots, u_n$, which are normalized in $[0, w_k]$. With this transformation, the AVF can be re-written in the following equivalent form:

$$V(\mathbf{x}) = \sum_{k=1}^{n} v_k(x_k) \tag{3.11}$$

With this model, a straightforward decision rule is to classify a borrower into the non-default class if $V(\mathbf{x}) > t$, where $0 < t < 1$ is a cut-off point defined in the value scale of the additive model.

The estimation of model (3.11) and the cut-off point t from a set of training data, can be expressed as an optimization problem, very similar to the ones presented in the previous sub-section:

$$\begin{array}{lll}
\min & \dfrac{1}{m_0}\sum_{i\in 0}\sigma_i + \dfrac{1}{m_1}\sum_{i\in 1}\sigma_i & \\
\text{subject to :} & V(\mathbf{x}_i) = \sum_{k=1}^{n} v_k(x_{ik}) & \text{for all borrowers} \\
& V(\mathbf{x}_i) + \sigma_i \geq t + \delta & \text{for non-defaulted borrowers} \\
& V(\mathbf{x}_i) - \sigma_i \leq t - \delta & \text{for defaulted borrowers} \\
& V(\mathbf{x}_*) = 0,\ V(\mathbf{x}^*) = 1 & \\
& v_k(x_{ik}) \geq v_k(x_{jk}) \geq 0 & \text{for all } i, j, k \text{ with } x_{ik} \geq x_{jk} \\
& \sigma_1, \ldots, \sigma_m, t \geq 0 &
\end{array} \tag{3.12}$$

This optimization formulation is very similar to (3.10), combined with the weighted objective function (3.11). Formulation (3.12), however, is based on a different type of modeling form (AVF instead of a linear decision function). The last two constraints define the scale and monotonicity of the AVF. For instance, $V(\mathbf{x}_*) = 0$, $V(\mathbf{x}^*) = 1$ ensure that the model is scaled in [0, 1], where $\mathbf{x}_* = (x_{1*}, \ldots, x_{n*})$ corresponds to the characteristics of the riskiest borrower and $\mathbf{x}^* = \left(x_1^*, \ldots, x_n^*\right)$ is a data vector representing the most creditworthy borrower. The monotonicity of the AVF is ensured through the constraints $v_k(x_{ik}) \geq v_k(x_{jk})$ for cases $x_{ik} \geq x_{jk}$, which ensure that the partial performance (credit score) of a borrower i on risk attribute k should be higher (i.e., better) that the score of other borrowers with worse characteristics.

Of course, to fully define the formulation of the problem (3.12) and solve it, an explicit expression for the marginal value functions $v_1(x_1), \ldots, v_n(x_n)$ is needed. One possibility is to use a pre-defined parametric form. However, if a non-linear form is selected, this will make problem (3.12) a non-linear programming problem (possibly non-convex, too), which would be difficult to solve. Alternatively, the marginal value functions can be assumed to have an arbitrary piecewise linear form. This makes the model much more flexible (a piecewise linear function can be linear, non-linear, convex, concave, etc.), and further allows the model to be fully derived from data through LP formulations, which are very easy to solve, even for large-scale data.

3.2.4.2 Outranking Models

The founding principles of outranking techniques can be traced to social choice theory. In contrast to the functional models employed in the context of MAVT, outranking models are expressed in relational form through which the validity of affirmations such as "alternative i is at least as good as (or preferred over) alternative j" can be analyzed. Exploiting such pairwise comparisons through appropriate procedures leads to the final evaluation results (i.e., choice of the best ways of action, ranking or classification of finite set of alternatives from the best to the worst ones).

For instance, in the context of the ELECTRE methods, the evaluation process is based on pairwise comparisons used to assess the strength of the outranking relation "alternative i is at least as good as alternative j" ($\mathbf{x}_i \, S \, \mathbf{x}_j$). The comparisons are performed at two stages. The first involves the concordance test, in which the strength of the indications supporting the outranking relation is assessed. This can be done through the following concordance index:

$$C\left(\mathbf{x}_i, \mathbf{x}_j\right) = \sum_{k=1}^{n} w_k c_k\left(x_{ik}, x_{jk}\right)$$

where $c_k(x_{ik}, x_{jk})$ is the partial concordance index for risk attribute k, defined such that:

$$c_k(x_{ik}, x_{jk}) = \begin{cases} 0 & \text{if } x_{ik} < x_{jk} - p_k \\ \dfrac{x_{ik} - x_{jk} + p_k}{p_k - q_k} & \text{if } x_{jk} - p_k \leq x_{ik} \leq x_{jk} - q_k \\ 1 & \text{if } x_{ik} > x_{jk} - q_k \end{cases}$$

where $q_k \geq p_k \geq 0$ are preference and indifference thresholds for risk attribute k. The case $C(\mathbf{x}_i, \mathbf{x}_j) = 1$ indicates that the outranking relation is clearly verified by all performance criteria, whereas the case $C(\mathbf{x}_i, \mathbf{x}_j) = 0$ indicates that there is no evidence to support the hypothesis that borrower i is at least as creditworthy as (i.e., outranks) borrower j.

At the second stage, the strength of the indications against the outranking relation is assessed through the calculation of a discordance index for each criterion:

$$d_k(x_{ik}, x_{jk}) = \begin{cases} 0 & \text{if } x_{ik} > x_{jk} - p_k \\ \dfrac{x_{ik} - x_{jk} + p_k}{p_k - v_k} & \text{if } x_{jk} - v_k \leq x_{ik} \leq x_{jk} - p_k \\ 1 & \text{if } x_{ik} < x_{jk} - v_k \end{cases}$$

The discordance indices examine the existence of veto conditions, in which the performance of borrower i may be too low in one or more risk attributes (i.e., $d_k(x_{ik}, x_{jk}) \approx 1$ for some k) and consequently it cannot be concluded that he/she is at least as creditworthy as borrower j, irrespective of the rest of the evaluation factors. The veto threshold $v_k \geq p_k$ defines the minimum difference $x_{jk} - x_{ik}$ above which veto applies on risk attribute k.

The combination of the two stages can be performed in different ways. For example, in ELECTRE methods the following credibility index is used:

$$\sigma(\mathbf{x}_i, \mathbf{x}_j) = C(\mathbf{x}_i, \mathbf{x}_j) \prod_{k \in \mathcal{F}} \frac{1 - d_k(x_{ik}, x_{jk})}{1 - C(\mathbf{x}_i, \mathbf{x}_j)}$$

where $\mathcal{F}$ is the set of performance criteria such that $d_k(x_{ik}, x_{jk}) > C(\mathbf{x}_i, \mathbf{x}_j)$. Credibility indices close to one indicate that the outranking relation $\mathbf{x}_i \, S \, \mathbf{x}_j$ is almost surely true, whereas $\sigma(\mathbf{x}_i, \mathbf{x}_j) \approx 0$ indicates that the relation cannot be verified. With this credibility index, the relation $\mathbf{x}_i \, S \, \mathbf{x}_j$ holds true if and only if $\sigma(\mathbf{x}_i, \mathbf{x}_j) \geq \lambda$, where $0.5 < \lambda \leq 1$ is a user-defined cut-off threshold. Thus, the following relations can be defined:

$$\begin{aligned} \text{Preference } (\mathbf{x}_i \succ \mathbf{x}_j) &: (\mathbf{x}_i \, S \, \mathbf{x}_j) \text{ and } (\text{not } \mathbf{x}_j \, S \, \mathbf{x}_i) \\ \text{Indifference } (\mathbf{x}_i \sim \mathbf{x}_j) &: (\mathbf{x}_i \, S \, \mathbf{x}_j) \text{ and } (\mathbf{x}_j \, S \, \mathbf{x}_i) \\ \text{Incomparability } (\mathbf{x}_i \, R \, \mathbf{x}_j) &: (\text{not } \mathbf{x}_i \, S \, \mathbf{x}_j) \text{ and } (\text{not } \mathbf{x}_j \, S \, \mathbf{x}_i) \end{aligned}$$

For the purposes of credit risk assessment, the most straightforward way to apply this outranking framework in a classification setting, is to compare the borrowers against boundary profiles defined to separate the risk classes, instead of performing pairwise comparisons as above. For instance, for a two-class credit rating/scoring and default prediction problem, a single boundary $\mathbf{r} = (r_1, r_2, \ldots, r_n)$ is defined to separate the high risk from the low risk borrowers on each risk attribute. In the more general setting where q risk grades are considered, $q - 1$ boundary profiles would be needed. To simply the exposition, we shall only cover the two-class case here.

Having defined the profile vector $\mathbf{r}$, all borrowers are compared against it and the outranking relations $\mathbf{x}_i\ S\ \mathbf{r}$ and $\mathbf{r}\ S\ \mathbf{x}_i$ are checked. If $\mathbf{x}_i \succ \mathbf{r}$, then borrower i is assigned to the low risk class (creditworthy borrowers), whereas the case $\mathbf{r} \succ \mathbf{x}_i$ indicates a high risk of default. Finally, the case $\mathbf{x}_i\ R\ \mathbf{r}$ implies that the risk level of borrower i is ambiguous. In such a case, if an optimistic perspective is adopted, then the borrower can be considered as low risk, whereas with a pessimistic approach the borrower should be considered as a high-risk client. Ambiguous assignments usually arise for borrowers with special characteristics, which deserve a closer examination by expert credit analysts.

The construction of outranking models is either based on expert judgment or data-driven optimization approaches. To implement the latter approach, however, one must consider the complex form of an outranking model, which makes it difficult to derive all the required parameters (weights, thresholds, profiles, λ, etc.) with standard optimization techniques. To overcome this difficulty, either some parameters should be fixed to enable the estimation of the others with analytical optimization tools (linear/non-linear programming) or heuristics and metaheuristics should be employed.

3.3 Performance Measures

The performance of a credit scoring and rating model is evaluated through validation (back-testing) procedures such as the ones described in the previous chapter. In this section, we describe performance measures that can be used to assess analytically the predictive power and information value of credit scoring and rating models.

3.3.1 Misclassification Costs

The most basic analytical way to describe the performance of a scoring and rating model is to analyze the expected cost of wrong recommendations that a model provides.

In the context of the base dichotomic classification setting assumed in this presentation, two types of error may arise. The first involves the classification of a creditworthy borrower in the default category (high risk borrowers), and will be denoted by $ND \rightarrow D$. Similarly, the opposite type of error can be defined ($D \rightarrow ND$) when high risk borrowers who will ultimately default, are considered as being creditworthy.

Each type of error has a cost for the lender (e.g., credit institution). More specifically, errors of the form $ND \rightarrow D$ are associated with opportunity costs, which arise when creditworthy customers are rejected. On the other hand, errors $D \rightarrow ND$ lead to capital losses from granting loans to borrowers who will not be able to meet their debt obligations. Denoting these costs by C_{ND} and C_D, respectively, the expected cost of a wrong decision can be expressed as follows:

$$E(C) = \pi_D \varepsilon_D C_D + \pi_{ND} \varepsilon_{ND} C_{ND} \tag{3.13}$$

where ε_D and ε_{ND} are the error rates for the two risk classes. In particular, ε_D represents the frequency of errors of the type $D \rightarrow ND$, whereas ε_{ND} is the frequency of errors of the type $ND \rightarrow D$.

In credit risk analysis, it generally holds that $C_D \gg C_{ND}$, i.e., the loss of accepting bad loans is usually much higher than the opportunity cost of rejecting good borrowers. Although the relationship between C_D and C_{ND} varies depending on the characteristics of the loan, as well as over time, and country/region, it is often the case that $C_D/C_{ND} > 10$.

3.3.2 *Classification Accuracies*

The most difficult issue in using the above expected cost as a performance measure, is that the costs C_D and C_{ND} are not easy to specify explicitly and they vary over time. A straightforward way to overcome this difficulty is to use performance measures that focus on the discriminating power and predictive accuracy of a credit scoring/rating model. In the remaining of the presentation, we cover such measures, assuming that a given credit scoring/rating model is tested on a sample of m_T borrowers, including m_T^D default instances and m_T^{ND} cases from the non-default category. This test sample is different from the training set used for model development.

The results of a binary credit scoring/rating model applied to such a test sample, can be summarized through a classification matrix (often referred to as the confusion matrix), such as the one in Table 3.2. The rows of the matrix correspond to the known (actual) status of the borrowers used to test the model and the columns correspond to the predictions (outputs) of the model. The entries of the matrix correspond to the combinations between actual data and prediction outcomes. For instance, *a* represents the number of defaulted borrowers classified by the model in

Table 3.2 Classification matrix

		Predictions	
		Default	Non-default
Actual	Default	a	b
status	Non-default	c	d

the same risk category, whereas b is the number of defaulted borrowers misclassified by the model to the non-default class. Thus, $a + b = m_T^D$ and $c + d = m_T^{ND}$.

From this matrix, the overall classification accuracy rate can be defined as $OCA = (a + d)/m_T$, i.e., the percentage of borrowers classified correctly to the total number of test instances. Similarly, accuracy rates can be defined for each risk group, separately. The accuracy rate for the default class is $A_D = a/m_T^D$ and the one for the non-default class is $A_{ND} = d/m_T^{ND}$.

The problem with using overall accuracy as a performance measure in credit risk analysis, is that it can easily lead to misleading conclusions. As already noted earlier, the number of defaults is usually quite low compared to non-defaults, which implies that $m_T^D \ll m_T^{ND}$. For instance, consider a sample of 1000 borrowers, which consists of 950 non-default instances and 50 default cases. A model that classifies correctly 900 of the non-defaulted and 25 of the defaulted borrowers (i.e., $a = 25$, $d = 900$), has the following accuracy rates:

$$OCA = 0.925 \quad A_D = 0.5 \quad A_{ND} = 0.9$$

It is obvious that the overall accuracy is quite high (925 correct predictions out of 1000), but this is not representative of the performance of the model across the two classes. In fact, the model is hardly acceptable when it comes to the identification of borrowers that are likely to default.

This issue can be addressed by considering the average of the class accuracy rates, instead of the overall accuracy. The average classification accuracy (ACA) rate is simply defined as $ACA = (A_D + A_{ND})/2$. In the above example, ACA is equal to 0.7, indicating a rather low performance of the model.

Of course, the use of ACA implicitly assumes that the two types of errors ($D \rightarrow ND$ and $ND \rightarrow D$) are equally important. This assumption appears, at first, unrealistic, if one takes under consideration that the costs of the two types of error are very different, i.e., $C_D \gg C_{ND}$. However, in credit risk analysis, one should also consider that the a priori probability of default (π_D) is much lower than 1, which implies that $\pi_D \ll \pi_{ND}$. For instance, π_D is usually around 5%. Therefore, when misclassification costs cannot be explicitly defined, it is rather reasonable to assume that $\pi_D C_D \approx \pi_{ND} C_{ND}$, which implies that the average error rate $(\varepsilon_D + \varepsilon_{ND})/2$, is a rather reasonable proxy for the expected cost $E(C)$, as defined in (3.13). Thus, in the context of credit risk modeling ACA may be a better measure that the standard OCA criterion. However, in both cases, one must make/accept assumptions about the underlying costs and prior probabilities, which may be not generally realistic, acceptable, or applicable. To address this limitation other performance measures can be considered.

3.3.3 Receiver Operating Characteristic Curve

The receiver operating characteristic (ROC) curve overcomes the limitations mentioned about for the use of accuracy rates and provides a more comprehensive assessment of the discriminating power of a scoring/rating model, without resorting to assumptions about costs or prior probabilities.

Given a scoring/rating model $f(\mathbf{x})$ that provides a credit score or a PD estimate, the classification matrix of Table 3.2 is constructed by specifying a cut-off score or probability that maps the outputs of the model to the two risk categories (default/non-default). The specification of this cut-off point is implicitly based on assumptions about the costs and the prior probabilities of default, as well as subjective judgment about the lending policy of the lender. For instance, a credit institution that seeks to increase its market share, may adopt a low cut-off point to increase the number of loans granted. As the number of accepted loans increases, the ratio of bad loans accepted to the total number of bad loans, also increases (i.e., the error rate ε_D). On the other hand, under crisis conditions, a bank adopts a high cut-off point, to minimize its risk exposure to bad loans, thus leading to lower error rate ε_D and higher error rate ε_{ND} (more good loans are rejected).

The ROC curve allows the measurement of the performance of a model across all cut-offs (low to high). More specifically, adopting the standard ROC terminology, we define the following true positive and false positive rates (TPR, FPR), as functions of the cut-off decision threshold t:

$$TPR(t) = \frac{d(t)}{m_T^{ND}} \qquad FPR(t) = \frac{b(t)}{m_T^D}$$

where $d(t)$ is the number of non-defaulted borrowers classified correctly with the cut-off threshold t, and $b(t)$ is the number of defaulted borrowers misclassified to the non-default class (again as a function of t). TPR is also referred to as sensitivity, whereas $1 - FPR$ is referred as specificity.

The ROC curve is a representation of (FPR, TPR) points over all choices for the cut-off threshold t. An illustrative example of a ROC curve is shown in Fig. 3.7. Starting with high values for t, both FPR and TPR are low, because a high cut-off threshold leads to the rejection of most loans. Increasing the cut-off point implies a less strict lending policy, where most loans are accepted. Thus, FPR and TPR both increase, but for the decision model to be meaningful, TPR should be higher than FPR. Otherwise most of the accepted loans would be bad. The diagonal dotted line corresponds to a model with no discriminating power, for which $TPR(t) = FPR(t)$, for all t. The recommendations of such a model could be considered as being made completely at random, thus providing no useful information about the true status of the borrowers.

The closer is the ROC curve to the upper left corner point (0, 1), the stronger is the model. This ideal point can be used to select the optimal cut-off point t^*. One approach is to find the cut-off point corresponding to a point on the ROC curve that is closest to the ideal:

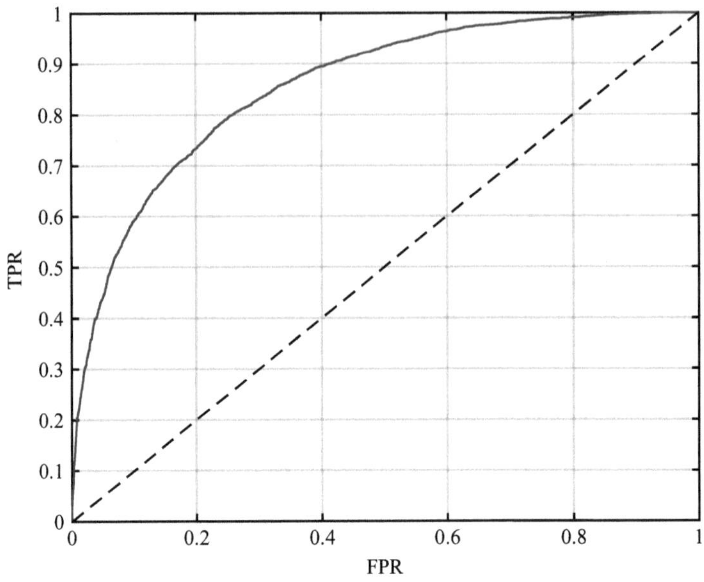

Fig. 3.7 A ROC curve

$$t^* = \text{argmin}_t \sqrt{[1 - TPR(t)]^2 + [FPR(t)]^2}$$

The area under the ROC curve (AUROC) is a standard measure for assessing the discriminating power of a scoring model. AUROC ranges between 0 and 1, with values closer to 1 indicating better performance. A model having AUROC≈0.5 is similar to a random model with no discriminating power. In Fig. 3.7 such a case corresponds to a ROC curve that is close to the diagonal.

AUROC also has a probabilistic interpretation. In fact, it represents the probability that a random borrower from the non-default class has a higher credit score that a random defaulted borrower. Thus, AUROC can be derived directly from the credit scores $f(\mathbf{x}_1), f(\mathbf{x}_2), \ldots, f(\mathbf{x}_{m_T})$ for a sample of m_T borrowers, as follows:

$$AUROC = \frac{1}{m_T^D m_T^{ND}} \sum_{i \in D, j \in ND} I_{ij}$$

where I_{ij} is defined as follows:

$$I_{ij} = \begin{cases} 1 & \text{if } f(\mathbf{x}_i) > f(\mathbf{x}_j) \\ 0.5 & \text{if } f(\mathbf{x}_i) = f(\mathbf{x}_j) \\ 0 & \text{if } f(\mathbf{x}_i) < f(\mathbf{x}_j) \end{cases}$$

A popular variant of the ROC curve for validating credit models, is the cumulative accuracy profile (CAP) curve. The CAP curve replaces the FPR with the acceptance rate (ACR), which represents the number of accepted borrowers (i.e., those with credit scores $f(\mathbf{x}) \geq t$) to the total number of test instances. In terms, of the elements of the classification matrix (Table 3.2), the acceptance rate is defined as $ACR(t) = [b(t) + d(t)]/m_T$. Thus, the CAP curve plots (ACR, TPR) pairs, for all cut-offs. The area under the CAP curve is known as the Gini index or accuracy ratio and it is closely related to AUROC. In fact, it can be shown that:

$$\text{Gini index} = 2AUROC - 1$$

3.3.4 Kolmogorov-Smirnov Distance

The Kolmogorov-Smirnov distance (KSD) is a statistical distance measure representing the maximum absolute difference between two cumulative distribution functions (CDFs). To define the KSD, let us assume that credit scores $f(\mathbf{x}_1), \ldots, f(\mathbf{x}_{m_T})$ are available for a set of m_T borrowers, and let their CDFs for the defaulted and non-defaulted categories be

$$F_D(t) = \frac{1}{m_T^D} \sum_{i=1}^{m_T^D} I[f(\mathbf{x}_i) \leq t] \qquad F_{ND}(t) = \frac{1}{m_T^{ND}} \sum_{i=1}^{m_T^{ND}} I[f(\mathbf{x}_i) \leq t]$$

where $I[\cdot]$ is an indicator function with $I[f(\mathbf{x}_i) \leq t] = 1$ if $f(\mathbf{x}_i) \leq t$, and $I[f(\mathbf{x}_i) \leq t] = 0$ if $f(\mathbf{x}_i) > t$. Then, the KSD is defined as the maximum absolute difference of the two CDFs:

$$KSD = \max_t |F_D(t) - F_{ND}(t)|$$

KSD ranges between 0 and 1, with higher values indicating a model with stronger discriminating performance. Figure 3.8 shows an illustrative example. The red (dotted) line represents the CDF for the credit scores among defaulted borrowers, whereas the solid (blue) line is the CDF for the non-defaulted borrowers. If higher credit scores correspond to lower probabilities of default, one would generally expect that $F_D(t) \geq F_{ND}(t)$, for every cut-off threshold t. This is the case shown in Fig. 3.8, where the red (dotted) line is above the blue (solid) line. The closer the two CDFs are, the less powerful is the credit scoring model.

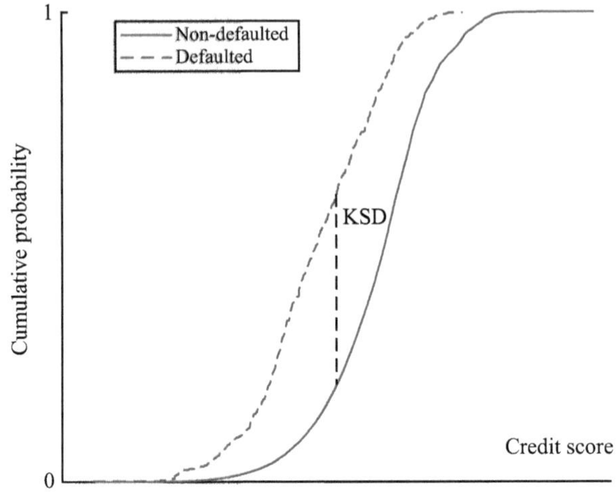

Fig. 3.8 Cumulative probability distributions of credit scores and the Kolmogorov-Smirnov distance

3.4 Notes and References

The analytical models for credit risk model have evolved considerably over the past decades, since the first work of Altman (1968) for bankruptcy prediction. During the 1970s and early 1980s, linear statistical models such as discriminant analysis and logistic regression dominated this field. Such models were mainly developed in the context of financial distress and bankruptcy prediction using corporate data. Some well-known works include the z-score model of Altman et al. (1977) and the logistic regression models of Ohlson (1980) and Zavgren (1985). A review of these early works in the context of bankruptcy prediction can be found in Dimitras et al. (1996). Logistic regression remains the main industry standard, due to its good statistical properties, the comprehensibility of linear models, and the analytical insights that it provides regarding the importance of the risk rating attributes.

During the 1980s and 1990s new techniques were explored, originating from data mining/machine learning and operations research. Moreover, as data availability for credit risk modeling started becoming more easily available, a lot of research focused not only on corporate financial distress, but also on credit risk assessment. Some early studies, include those of Frydman et al. (1985) who introduced a rule-based approach, and Srinivasan and Kim (1987) who examined various techniques, including mathematical programming, classification trees, and MCDA, in the context of credit granting, as well as the study of Tabouratzi et al. (2017) who examined distress characteristics in Greek manufacturing small and medium-sized enterprises. Neural networks and related techniques became quite popular during the 1990s and early 2000s. Some typical early works on the use of such models in credit risk assessment include those of Desai et al. (1996), Galindo and Tamayo (2000), Piramuthu (1999), and West (2000). Given the complexity of such computational models and their lack of transparency/comprehensibility, Baesens et al. (2003) were among the first to examine ways addressing this shortcoming (see also, Martens et al. 2007). MCDA methods for credit risk modeling, including value function models and outranking techniques, have been considered in several studies, such as those of Bugera et al. (2002), Doumpos et al. (2002), Doumpos and Pasiouras (2005), Doumpos and Zopounidis (2011), and Zhang et al. (2014), among others.

Empirical results on the performance of various models for credit risk scoring and rating have been presented on various studies such as Lessmann et al. (2015) and Papageorgiou et al. (2008), whereas Blöchlinger and Leippold (2006) and Oliver (2013) discuss issues related to the performance of credit scoring models, covering not only statistical measures, but also economic/financial criteria.

Chapter 4
Applications to Corporate Default Prediction and Consumer Credit

4.1 Introduction

This chapter illustrates the use of analytical descriptive and predictive techniques for credit risk assessment. More specifically, two applications are presented. The first involves the prediction of corporate defaults using a cross-country sample of European firms. Predictive models combining financial data are developed using methodologies, such as the ones described in Chap. 3. The performance of the models is assessed through statistical performance criteria focusing on the accuracy of the models' outputs. The contributions of the financial variables in the models is also discussed.

The second application focus on a retail banking problem, involving risk assessment in credit card loans. The analysis in this case is based on a descriptive methodology, which can be used to obtain insights into the characteristics of the data and identify cases characterized by common patterns. More specifically, cluster analysis is used to derive clusters (groups) of customers with similar risk profile and features.

The integrated use of such techniques (predictive and descriptive) is fundamental for credit risk modeling. Descriptive analyses facilitate the understanding of the data, thus helping the analyst to construct improved decision models that better fit different parts/segments and aspects of the problem.

4.2 Prediction of Corporate Defaults

The prediction of corporate failures and defaults is an important part of corporate credit rating models. In this section we illustrate the development of predictive models for corporate default prediction, using techniques such as the ones presented

M. Doumpos et al., *Analytical Techniques in the Assessment of Credit Risk*, EURO Advanced Tutorials on Operational Research,
https://doi.org/10.1007/978-3-319-99411-6_4

in the previous chapter. This has been an active area of research not only in corporate finance, but also in fields involved with analytical modeling, such as OR/MS and computer science.

For the purposes of the analysis presented in this section, we consider corporate default in a broad setting that refers to situations where firms face, systematically, serious losses and/or become insolvent with their liabilities. These may involve, among others:

- Unpaid debts to suppliers and employees
- Unpaid preferred dividends
- Overdraft of bank deposits
- Actual or potential damages from litigation
- Missed principal or interest payments under borrowing agreements (default)

Except for credit risk modeling and assessment, models for predicting corporate defaults are highly important in several other contexts. For instance, default risk estimates are of interest to investors and asset managers for investment planning and capital allocation decisions. Shareholders and corporate management may also use the outputs of default prediction models for making strategic and operational decisions regarding the financing and dividend policy of firms. Moreover, default prediction models provide policy makers with early warning systems that can be used to design and take actions to ensure financial stability.

Similarly to credit risk assessment and relevant approaches described in Chaps. 1 and 2, default prediction models consider various types of information regarding the financial status of a firm, its operation and business activity, the external environment, as well as market data for listed companies.

For the purposes of the analysis in this section we focus on financial data derived from publicly available financial statements. This is the most basic and fundamental information for corporate default prediction and credit risk assessment that is universally applicable to almost all types of firms (listed/unlisted, small/large, etc.). The presented application covers issues like data collection, variables' selection, and comparative analysis of different types of analytical approaches for predictive modeling.

4.2.1 Data Description

The data used for this application were obtained from the ORBIS database, which provides detailed information on over 50 million European companies. The sample involves 13,414 European from six countries, during the period 2009–2011. The firms in the sample are small and medium-sized enterprises (SMEs) from the manufacturing sector. For this analysis a SME is defined according to Eurostat's definition, i.e., 50–250 employees, 10–50 million euros in sales, and 10–43 million euros in total assets.

Table 4.1 Sample observations by year, category, and country

	2009		2010		2011		Total	
Countries	D	ND	D	ND	D	ND	D	ND
Belgium	10	549	16	519	7	434	33	1502
France	46	1063	86	1075	49	1140	181	3278
Germany	6	1006	16	1000	8	839	30	2845
Italy	130	3398	135	3245	376	3091	641	9734
Spain	88	1377	87	1288	70	1140	245	3805
UK	10	1102	10	1239	11	1210	31	3551
Total	290	8495	350	8366	521	7854	1161	24,715

Table 4.2 Default rates (in %) by year and country

	2009	2010	2011	Total
Belgium	1.79	2.99	1.59	2.15
France	4.15	7.41	4.12	5.23
Germany	0.59	1.57	0.94	1.04
Italy	3.68	3.99	10.85	6.18
Spain	6.01	6.33	5.79	6.05
UK	0.90	0.80	0.90	0.87
Total	3.30	4.02	6.22	4.49

Using the information available in ORBIS, the firms were classified into two groups, one consisting of defaulted firms and a second group of non-defaulted cases. Default firms were identified according to their status records in the ORBIS database, as those with default in payments, in bankruptcy proceedings, in liquidation, as well as firms in receivership. All other active firms were used to compile the non-defaulted group. Overall, the sample includes 24,715 firm-year observations in the non-defaulted class and 1161 defaulted cases.

To enable the development and testing of predictive models, the data were divided into two distinct parts, namely a training and a testing sample. The models are constructed (fitted) using the training data and their classification performance is analyzed based on the testing sample. Generally, one can adopt different approaches to implement a training-testing scheme for assessing the performance of distress rating models. In order to adopt a realistic approach, the evaluation of the model should be done in a future period. Following this procedure, the training sample consists of data from the period 2009–2010 whereas the test sample covers the subsequent period (i.e., the year 2011).

Overall, the training data consist of 17,501 observations, including 16,861 non-defaulted observations and 640 defaulted instances. The test sample includes the remaining 7854 non-defaulted and 521 defaulted observations.

Table 4.1 presents some details about the composition of the sample by the status of the firms (defaulted-D, non-defaulted-ND), country, and year. Table 4.2 presents similar information about the default rates (i.e., the percentage of defaulted cases to the total number of firms for each combination of country and year). It is evident that most of the firms come from Italy (40%), followed by Spain. In both these countries SMEs play a major role in the countries' business activity and economic status. The overall default rate increased from 3.3% in 2009 to 6.22% in 2011. This increase over the three years is a clear indication of the impact that the global crisis of 2007–2008 and the subsequent European debt crisis, had on the viability of European SMEs. This is most noticeable for Italian SMEs, where the sample default rate increased from 3.68% in 2009 to more than 10.8% in 2011. For the other countries, there is an increase in 2010, followed by a decrease in 2011. Finally, it is worth noting that the default rates in Germany and UK are significantly lower than the rest of the countries.

4.2.2 Selection of Variables

The use of financial information in credit rating models and default prediction is very common, due to the availability of financial data. However, the choice of the appropriate financial indicators to assess the strengths and weaknesses of a firm is a challenging issue. Typically, these indicators are expressed in the form of ratios representing meaningful relationships between financial data about corporate profitability, solvency, liquidity, and managerial efficiency. As explained in Sect. 2.4.1, there are several financial ratios that can be derived using data from corporate financial statements (e.g., balance sheet, income statement). While judgmental (expert-based) rating systems may consider a wide range of ratios (combined with other information), analytical predictive models are usually based on a handful data predictor variables, to ensure that the models are easy to use and update, while eliminating statistical problems (e.g., multicollinearity) that arise when combining multiple interrelated variables into a predictive model. Thus, there is a tradeoff between using a small set of predictors and making sure that all relevant information is embodied into the model without adding overlapping information that could overfit the training data but provide poor generalizing performance.

Having in mind the above remarks, for this application we consider a compact set of financial ratios selected based on their relevance for credit risk assessment and default prediction according to the literature in this area. More specifically, two specifications are considered, as shown in Table 4.3. The first specification A involves four financial ratios, whereas the second (specification B) considers seven ratios. For all ratios, Table 4.3 shows their relation to default and credit risk. Ratios for which a negative relationship is defined, reduce the risk of default, in the sense that higher values for these ratios are expected to improve the financial strength and creditworthiness of the firms. Profitability ratios, such as return on assets (ROA) is a typical example: as ROA increases, the risk of failure and default gets lower (and vice versa). On the other hand, ratios that are positively related to default risk represent risk factors, in the sense that higher values for these ratios are indicators

Table 4.3 Description of financial ratios

	Definition	Relation to default
Specification A		
Return on assets (ROA)	Earnings before taxes/Total assets	–
Debt ratio	Total liabilities/Total assets	+
Quick ratio	(Cash + Accounts receivable)/Current liabilities	–
Credit collection period	(Accounts receivable/Total revenues)×360	+
Specification B		
Return on assets (ROA)	Earnings before taxes/Total assets	–
EBITDA margin	Earnings before depreciation, interest and taxes/Total revenues	–
Debt ratio	Total liabilities/Total assets	+
Interest cover	Earnings before interest and taxes/Financial expenses	–
Quick ratio	(Cash + Accounts receivable)/Current liabilities	–
Credit collection period	(Accounts receivable/Total revenues)×360	+
Earnings per employee	Earnings before taxes/Number of Employees	–

of higher risk. The debt ratio is such an example: firms relying heavily on debt have high debt ratio, which indicates a high risk of default.

Specification A involves four financial ratios, each covering a different aspect of the financial operation and performance of firms. ROA is the most widely used profitability ratio. It compares net income (excluding taxes) to the assets of the firms (i.e., the means used for the operation of a firm). ROA is extensively used in corporate finance as the main indicator to assess the global profitability of firms. Several studies have shown that it has strong predictive power for credit risk measurement and default prediction for different types of firms and regions. The debt ratio is a common solvency indicator representing the debt burden of firms. Low levels typically represent a healthy capital structure, whereas high levels are associated with excessive debt. Quick ratio is a liquidity indicator that focuses on assets that are generally liquid (cash and accounts receivable), excluding stock (inventories), which may take time to generate cash for a firm. Liquidity is an important factor for the financial strength of manufacturing firms and SMEs, such as the firms considered in this application. Finally, the credit collection period enables the assessment of managerial efficiency from the perspective of the credit policy that a firm follows towards its customers. Firms with slow account receivable turnover (i.e., high credit collection period) may face liquidity problems due to the extensive credit period they provide to their customers.

In addition to the above four core ratios, specification B considers three additional ratios. More specifically, EBITDA margin is used as an additional profitability

Table 4.4 Correlations between the financial ratios

	Return on assets	EBITDA margin	Debt ratio	Interest cover	Liquidity ratio	Credit collection
EBITDA margin	0.81					
Debt ratio	−0.43	−0.40				
Interest cover	0.52	0.38	−0.36			
Liquidity ratio	0.29	0.24	−0.56	0.30		
Credit collection	−0.13	−0.04	0.17	−0.09	0.13	
Earnings/employee	0.89	0.78	−0.41	0.48	0.30	−0.07

indicator focusing on the operating income of a firm (earnings before depreciation, interest and taxes) in comparison to total revenues. Interest cover is also considered to examine the debt servicing ability of the firms; it represents the coverage of financial expenses through a firm's earnings before interest and taxes. Finally, the earnings per employee ratio is used as an additional managerial efficiency indicator focusing on the human resources of a firm.

Using both specifications in the analysis enables the examination of the robustness of the results to the selection of different predictors and the investigation of the added value of using a more comprehensive set of financial data for predicting corporate defaults.

Table 4.4 summarizes the correlations between the financial ratios. As expected profitability ratios are strongly (positively) related to each other. Moreover, it is evident that higher debt is associated with lower profitability, whereas liquidity is positively related with profitability and has a negative association with the debt burden of the firms. The interest cover ability of the firms improves with profitability and is affected negatively by higher debt. Finally, regarding the credit policy of the firms, the correlations show that more extended credit collection periods are associated with lower profitability and higher debt, although these relationships are generally weak. These correlation results support the definition of the abovementioned two specifications for the variables considered in the analysis. Indeed, specification A consists of four variables covering different aspects of the firms' financial performance, generally characterized by low to moderate correlations. Specification B, on the other hand, includes more variables with higher correlations. More complex, non-linear models may benefit from a richer set of variables leading to better results, whereas one generally expects marginal differences when introducing highly correlated to simpler linear models.

Table 4.5 presents the average values of all ratios for both classes of firms (D for the defaulted class, ND for the non-defaulted cases). It can be easily verified that these class averages are in accordance with the remarks made earlier about the

Table 4.5 Averages of the financial ratios by the status of the firms

	D	ND
Return on assets	−11.09	5.86
EBITDA margin	−5.73	7.92
Debt ratio	0.87	0.57
Interest cover	1.81	16.22
Liquidity ratio	0.52	0.98
Credit collection period	110.02	82.20
Earnings per employee	−18.12	11.71

Table 4.6 Averages of the financial ratios by the status of the firms and country

	Status	BEL	FRA	DEU	ITA	ESP	GBR
Return on assets	D	−13.98	−10.25	−4.34	−11.50	−11.57	−7.00
	ND	5.90	5.85	6.95	5.45	5.29	6.74
Debt ratio	D	0.83	0.77	0.68	0.90	0.88	0.83
	ND	0.57	0.57	0.55	0.58	0.56	0.58
Liquidity ratio	D	0.55	0.54	0.44	0.49	0.60	0.55
	ND	1.02	0.98	1.05	0.95	1.00	0.98
Credit collection period	D	77.49	74.24	34.75	123.43	121.35	59.50
	ND	76.52	78.26	68.52	88.98	85.22	77.36
EBITDA margin	D	−6.84	−4.68	1.88	−6.08	−6.77	−2.52
	ND	8.13	7.32	8.20	7.88	7.81	8.41
Interest cover	D	0.36	1.68	3.54	2.24	0.42	4.54
	ND	15.75	16.72	16.01	15.11	16.02	19.42
Earnings per employee	D	−19.96	−12.59	−6.12	−20.28	−18.74	−10.53
	ND	12.09	11.60	12.56	11.47	10.72	12.69

relationship of the selected ratios with default risk. Indeed, non-defaulted firms are more profitable, they have higher interest coverage, lower debt, higher liquidity, faster receivables turnover, and stronger profitability per employee. The differences between the two classes were tested through parametric and non-parametric tests (t-test, Mann-Whitney test) and were all found significant at the 99% confidence level.

Table 4.6 provides additional information about the class averages of the predictors for each country separately. From the results shown in this illustration, it is interesting to observe that non-defaulted firms exhibit similar behavior across all countries, as there no striking differences are observed in the country averages for the non-defaulted group (with an exception regarding the credit collection period in Italy and Spain, which is higher than the rest of the countries). Regarding the defaulted firms, some differences are evident, mainly regarding Germany and the United Kingdom, but this can be due to the small number of defaulted firms from these countries in the sample.

4.2.3 Analytical Approaches for Predictive Modeling

For the development of models to predict default using the data described above, three popular methods are used from the ones described in Chap. 3. More specifically, we use logistic regression (Sect. 3.2.1), support vector machines (Sect. 3.2.3), and the UTADIS multicriteria method (Sect. 3.2.4).

Logistic regression (LR) is a widely used statistical approach for the development of credit risk assessment (scoring/rating) and default prediction models. It is the most commonly used method and it is often used as a benchmark for the comparison of advanced techniques.

Support vector machines (SVMs) have become an increasingly popular non-parametric methodology for developing classification and regression models. SVMs provide models in linear and non-linear form using model fitting criteria that consider both the fitting ability of the models as well as their complexity. In this analysis we use both linear and non-linear SVMs. Non-linear models are constructed by mapping the data to a high dimensional space through a kernel function, namely the radial basis function (RBF) kernel, which is defined as follows:

$$K(\mathbf{x}_i, \mathbf{x}_j) = \exp\left(-\frac{\|\mathbf{x}_i - \mathbf{x}_j\|^2}{2\sigma^2}\right)$$

where σ is a user-defined constant representing the width of the RBF kernel. The specification of this parameter was performed through cross-validation. For the construction of the SVM models the data were normalized to zero mean and unit variance, thus eliminating the effect that the different scales of the predictor variables have on the calculation of the kernel function.

Finally, the UTADIS method, a popular multicriteria method for constructing classification models, leads to the development of an additive value function that is used to score the firms and decide upon their classification. The additive function is monotone with respect to the decision attributes (i.e., the predictors) and its developed using linear programming.

4.2.4 Results

4.2.4.1 The Contribution of the Predictors in the Models

We start the presentation and analysis of the results with an examination of the contribution of the financial ratios in the models constructed through the three methods mentioned above. Understanding the way that input variables are used in a predictive model and how they contribute to the model's outputs is an important issue in credit risk modeling and financial decision-making, in general. Model comprehensibility and interpretability issues have recently attracted much interest among researchers, practitioners, and supervisors. Complex models are usually difficult to understand their underlying structure, thus operating as "black boxes" and raising issues regarding their practical use. Simpler modeling forms, on the other hand, offer transparency, enabling the analyst to get insights into the decision attributes and the way the relate to the outcomes of a model.

In the present analysis, we examine the above issue through the two linear models developed with LR, linear SVMs (LSVM), and the additive model of the UTADIS method. The non-linear structure of the SVM model with the RBF kernel, makes the derivation of insights about the attributes, much more challenging and consequently it is omitted from this discussion. The linear models of LR and LSVM provide information about the coefficients of the financial ratios in the constructed linear prediction function. In the current setup, variables with positive coefficients are those that improve the creditworthiness of the firms and reduce the risk of default. On the other hand, as explained in Sect. 3.2.4, the additive model of the UTADIS multicriteria method is a weighted average of partial performance scores (default/credit risk scores for each financial ratio). The weights of the financial ratios in this weighted aggregation, are non-negative and sum-up to one, acting as proxies of the relative importance of the predictors in the model.

Table 4.7 presents the results regarding the coefficients of the financial ratios to the LR and LSVM models as well as the weights in the multicriteria model. The signs of the coefficients in the LR and LSVM models have the expected signs. For instance, ROA has a positive sign in both models, thus indicating that the viability and creditworthiness of the firms improve as their profitability increases. On the other hand, the coefficients of the debt ratio are negative, implying that high debt reduces the viability of the firms (i.e., default/credit risk increase).

It should be noted that the coefficients of the financial ratios in the LR models are not directly comparable to each other, because the ratios have different scales. However, similarly to standard regression models, the coefficient estimates in LR are associated with hypotheses tests regarding their statistical significance. In the

Table 4.7 Contribution of variables

	LR	LSVM	UTADIS
Specification A			
ROA	0.120	1.096	0.655
Debt ratio	−1.398	−0.289	0.038
Liquidity ratio	1.359	0.913	0.257
Credit collection period	−0.011	−0.433	0.050
Specification B			
ROA	0.057	0.627	0.084
EBITDA margin	0.037	0.181	0.114
Debt Ratio	−1.227	−0.256	0.037
Interest cover	0.010	0.035	0.039
Liquidity ratio	1.423	1.005	0.287
Collection period	−0.012	−0.482	0.065
Earnings per employee	0.018	0.346	0.370

present analysis all coefficients in both LR models were found statistically significant at the 1% level.

The LSVM model is non-parametric and consequently statistical hypothesis tests about the coefficients are not available. However, given that the data have been standardized to zero mean and unit variance, the magnitude of the coefficients can be used as an approximate proxy of the contribution of each ratio in the model. In that regard it is evident that profitability (ROA) and liquidity are the most important factors under both specifications A and B.

Regarding the additive model developed with the UTADIS method, it must be noted that it is, by definition, monotone with respect to the inputs, i.e., increasing for profit-related attributes and decreasing for attributes in minimization form, such as the debt ratio. Under specification A, ROA appears to be the most important attribute in the multicriteria model with a weight of 0.655, followed by liquidity. Liquidity is also an important attribute in the alternative specification B, whereas the weight of ROA is much lower as earnings per employee and EBITDA margin enter the model as alternative profitability measures.

Overall, the findings from the above results highlight the importance of profitability and liquidity as the main factors for assessing default and credit risk for this analysis. This makes sense, because the firms considered in the sample are SMEs and profitability/liquidity issues are indeed crucial for their successful operation. Such insights provide credit analysts and financial decision makers with important information regarding the underlying structure of predictive models, their economic/business sense, constituting a solid basis for adding domain knowledge into the analysis. Incorporating domain (expert) knowledge into data analytics techniques has been found in several studies to improve their robustness and generalizing performance of predictive models.

4.2.4.2 Classification Performance

The assessment of the predictive performance of all models is done using different metrics. The first one involves the accuracy rate, which, as explained in Sect. 3.3.2 refers the percentage of cases classified correctly by a model. Table 4.8 presents the results for the models used in the present application, for the out-of-sample holdout (test) cases (year 2011). The accuracy rates are reported separately for each class of firms (defaulted, non-defaulted). Moreover, the overall and average accuracy rates are also reported. The former represents the total number of correct predictions, whereas the latter is the mean of the individual accuracy rates for the two classes of firms. The rationale of the mean accuracy rate and its assumptions in terms of the expected misclassification costs were explained in Sect. 3.3.2.

The accuracies for specification A, range around 76–77% for the non-defaulted group, whereas for defaulted cases accuracy ranges around 85–89%. The mean accuracy ranges around 82%, whereas the overall is lower, around 77%, due to the different sizes of the two class of firms (the number of non-defaulted firms is much greater than defaulted firms). The differences between the methods are rather

Table 4.8 Accuracy rates (mean and overall accuracies)

	ND	D	Mean	Overall
Specification A				
LR	0.770	0.850	0.810	0.775
UTADIS	0.771	0.864	0.817	0.776
SVM	0.768	0.856	0.812	0.773
SVM-RBF	0.759	0.888	0.823	0.767
Specification B				
LR	0.769	0.866	0.817	0.775
UTADIS	0.773	0.860	0.816	0.778
SVM	0.766	0.867	0.816	0.770
SVM-RBF	0.763	0.894	0.828	0.771

Table 4.9 Area under the receiver operating characteristic curve

Methods	Overall	Belgium	France	Germany	Italy	Spain	UK
Specification A							
LR	**0.897**	**0.903**	0.883	**0.774**	0.887	0.914	0.823
UTADIS	0.895	**0.903**	0.866	0.710	**0.889**	0.903	0.780
LSVM	**0.897**	0.889	0.883	**0.774**	0.887	0.914	0.821
SVM-RBF	**0.897**	0.858	**0.889**	0.750	0.884	0.905	**0.846**
Specification B							
LR	0.896	0.889	0.881	**0.793**	0.883	0.910	0.832
UTADIS	0.894	**0.906**	0.872	0.725	0.885	0.900	**0.842**
LSVM	0.897	0.899	0.881	0.785	0.885	0.910	0.826
SVM-RBF	**0.899**	0.873	**0.894**	0.782	**0.888**	**0.914**	0.836

marginal, with UTADIS performing slightly better overall (due to its superior performance for the larger group of non-defaults). The non-linear SVM model (SVM-RBF), on the other hand, is more accurate for the class of defaulted firms as well as in terms of the mean accuracy rate. The accuracies rates for the second specification of the predictor variables, are very similar to the ones of specification A.

Another popular performance metric is the area under the receiver operating characteristic curve (AUROC, cf. Sect. 3.3.3), which enables the analysis of the predictive performance of classification rules under different hypotheses with respect to the misclassification costs and the a-priory class membership probabilities. Table 4.9 summarizes the AUROC results. Except for the overall performance of the classifiers, additional results are also reported for each country. The best performances in each case are marked in bold. Overall, the AUROC ranges around 90% under both specifications for the variables. This result, together with the similar results for the two specifications in terms of the accuracy rate, indicates that the compact set of four variables used in specification A provides a very good description for the risk of failure for the considered sample of European SMEs. Regarding

Table 4.10 Kolmogorov- Smirnov Results

Methods	Overall	Belgium	France	Germany	Italy	Spain	UK
Specification A							
LR	0.648	**0.666**	**0.692**	**0.559**	0.632	0.705	**0.626**
UTADIS	0.671	0.624	0.603	0.438	0.642	0.676	0.454
LSVM	0.646	0.664	0.668	0.544	0.634	**0.706**	0.617
SVM-RBF	**0.678**	0.629	0.682	0.547	**0.664**	0.683	0.612
Specification B							
LR	0.638	**0.700**	0.671	**0.529**	0.622	0.677	0.607
UTADIS	0.660	0.618	0.602	0.355	0.616	0.677	0.583
LSVM	0.646	0.687	0.673	0.515	0.629	0.694	**0.624**
SVM-RBF	**0.676**	0.671	**0.690**	0.519	**0.678**	**0.718**	0.623

specific counties, for most countries there are no significant differences in terms of the AUROC. However, for Germany and the UK, the results appear to be worse, but this may be due to the small samples of defaulted firms from these two countries. For Germany, the AUROC under specification A ranges between 71% and 78% but improves with the addition of more variables (specification B). A similar behavior is also observed for the UK.

The last performance measure used is the K-S test or Kolmogorov-Smirnov (KS) distance (cf. Sect. 3.3.4). The Kolmogorov-Smirnov distance is defined as the maximum difference between the cumulative distributions of the default/credit scores for the two groups of firms. A large positive difference (i.e., close to one) indicates that the scores assigned to the defaulted cases concentrate to the lower part of the scoring scale, whereas the scores of the non-defaulted cases are concentrated to higher levels of the evaluation scale.

Table 4.10 presents the results for the K-S measure. The results in both specifications are quite satisfactory. This means that the examined models can accurately separate the two classes of firms. For the full sample (column "Overall") K-S ranges between 0.638 and 0.678, with the non-linear SVM model (SVM-RBF) and UTADIS performing best, followed by linear SVM and logistic regression. Regarding the country-level results, the performance of the models for German SMEs is much lower than the rest of the countries, similarly to the observation made above for the AUROC measure.

4.3 Retail Banking

The retail banking plays a central role to the operation of commercial banks, providing basic banking services (loans and deposits) to individual consumers rather than corporate clients (wholesale banking). In recent years, banks have been striving to develop the retail sector by extending their products and services portfolios, improving the quality and response times for customer services, providing direct and indirect benefits to their clients, and strengthening their flexibility and adaptability to the changing needs of the customers.

At the same time, banks have established the idea of a package of services and look for opportunities to create a lifelong relationship with their client base while increasing their share in the consumer-client wallet. Taking advantage of the opportunity to expand the business and thus increase the profits offered by private customers requires:

1. the choice of a long-term policy,
2. the orientation of the business towards the needs and requirements of an ever-changing market,
3. controlling the elements that affect the operating and production costs,
4. personnel training in retail banking products and services.

Moreover, based on a bank's role in offering services, whether it acquires a debt (e.g., a loan) or creates a debt (e.g., a deposit) or undertakes a specific project (e.g. sending funds), we distinguish between active, passive and mediatory roles.

(a) Active Role

The granting of all types of loans creates a lender-borrower relationship. The status of the lender is the bank which acquires a claim for the return of the funds from the borrower. The total funds provided by the bank as part of its financial activity are receivables and are recorded in the assets of its balance sheet; for this purpose and we call these operations "active".

(b) Passive Role

The term "passive operations" is linked to a depositor-bank relationship, in which the bank acts as a debtor of the funds held in the depositor's account and must repay them to the beneficiary at the agreed time and with the interest agreed. From the accounting point of view, the debts of the bank are recorded in the liabilities of its balance sheet and are called "passive operations".

(c) Mediation Role

During mediation, the bank does not have the status of either the debtor or the lender of funds. It simply mediates a transaction without managing capital but providing its know-how, use of the branch network, electronic equipment, etc. For this mediatory task the bank receives the appropriate remuneration.

Nowadays there is a wide range of retail banking products and services, including savings accounts, personal loans, mortgages, credit and debit cards. The presentation in this chapter focuses on credit risk assessment for credit card loans. Nowadays, credit cards are widely used for consumer transactions and over the past decades they facilitated credit growth. As far as banks are concerned, high interest rates on credit cards, as well as commissions from affiliated companies, make credit cards a very attractive financial product. However, risks do exist, and even though they are not associated with extreme events, their frequency makes them important for retail banking. On the one hand, the use of credit cards is frequently associated with fraudulent transactions. On the other hand, the ease of access to credit cards and their extensive use often creates excessive debt burden for consumers that do not have the ability to meet their obligations.

With these remarks in mind, in the remainder of the chapter the use of data analytic techniques will be presented for the analysis of credit card data in terms of the credit risk. Cluster analysis will be used as the main analytical methodology. The next subsection briefly introduces cluster analysis, before proceeding with the presentation of the case data and the discussion of the results.

4.3.1 Clustering Techniques

In contrast to the techniques described in Chap. 3, clustering in an unsupervised approach for extracting knowledge from data by discovering unknown patterns from unstructured data. Clustering facilitate the organization of the data through the identification of groups (clusters) of observation characterized by similar characteristics. Each clustering algorithm has two main components. The first involves the process through which the clusters formed whereas the second is related to the metrics used to define the similarity between the objects under consideration.

Regarding the former distinction, hierarchical and partitioning clustering algorithms can be identified. Hierarchical clustering refers to the organization of the data into nested clusters, which are organized in a hierarchical tree structure. Hierarchical clustering starts by considering each case observation as a separate cluster (i.e., each cluster initially consists of a single instance). The most similar pair of clusters is then identified, and they are merged into a new (joined) cluster. Then, all distances between the clusters are updated and the process is repeated, until all objects are grouped into a single cluster. The outputs of this process can be illustrated through a hierarchical dendrogram structure, such as the one shown in Fig. 4.1. The horizontal axis corresponds to the instance in the data set, whereas the vertical axis represents the distance between clusters. The dendrogram structure shows how the elementary instances are grouped hierarchically into clusters. Clusters at the lower levels are the most similar ones, whereas clusters formed at higher levels of the hierarchy are more dissimilar. At the top, a single cluster consisting of the whole data set is formed. This bottom-up approach is commonly referred to as agglomerative clustering. A top-down approach (i.e., divisive clustering) can also be employed.

In contrast to hierarchical approaches, partitioning algorithms provide a grouping of the data observations into block clusters, whose number is usually predefined. In such approaches, objects can move in or out of groups at different stages of the analysis. Initially, some arbitrary cluster centers are selected, and the objects are distributed to the nearest centers, which correspond to the centers of the objects in the already formed groups. Then, an object is assigned to a new cluster if it is closer to the center of that cluster than the center of the cluster that it currently belongs to. The clusters closest to each other are unified, other groups are subdivided, etc. This process continues repeatedly until balance is reached, with a final set number of cluster-groups.

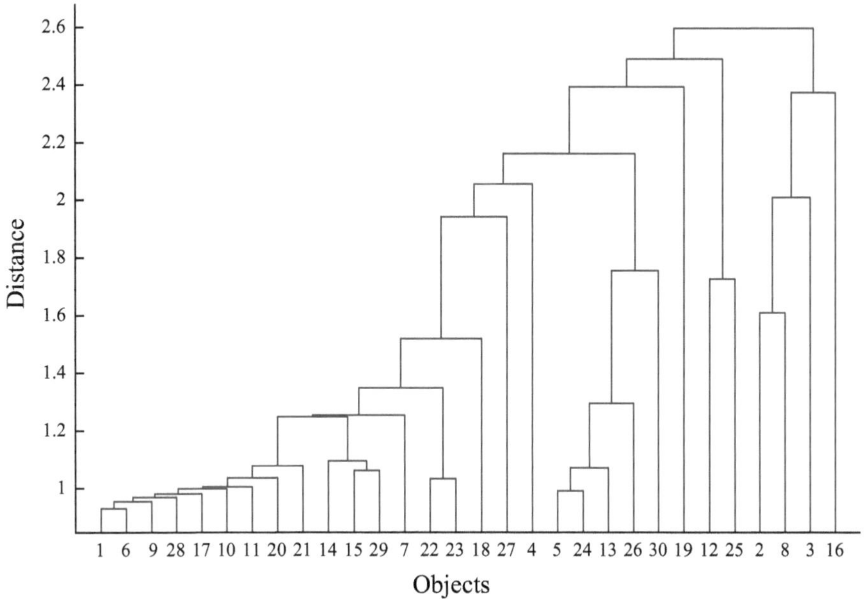

Fig. 4.1 Example of hierarchical clustering in a dendrogram structure

The most popular algorithm belonging to this class is the k-means clustering algorithm. The term k-means describes an algorithm that assigns each object to the cluster that has the closest means. The basic idea is to calculate centroids, one for each group. The best way to optimize these is to select them with the maximum possible distance between them. Next, each object is placed in the cluster with the nearest center point. Then, the cluster centers are updated, and the objects are again assigned according to the closest center. In this way, a loop is created, the result of which is to change the positions of the centers iteratively until no other changes are made.

Given a group of observations ($\mathbf{x}_1$, $\mathbf{x}_2$, ..., $\mathbf{x}_m$), where each observation is a n-dimension vector, k-means clustering leads to the identification of k groups, $\mathbf{S} = \{S_1, S_2, \ldots, S_k\}$, to minimize the following objective function:

$$\min \sum_{\ell=1}^{k} \sum_{\mathbf{x}_i \in S_\ell} D(\mathbf{x}_i, \boldsymbol{\mu}_\ell)$$

where $D(\mathbf{x}_i, \boldsymbol{\mu}_\ell)$ is a distance function between an object $\mathbf{x}_i$ and the center $\boldsymbol{\mu}_\ell$ of cluster ℓ. Popular choices for the distance function, include the Euclidean distance (and its squared form) and the Manhattan distance:

- Euclidean distance: $\|\mathbf{x}_i - \boldsymbol{\mu}_\ell\|$
- Squared Euclidean distance: $\|\mathbf{x}_i - \boldsymbol{\mu}_\ell\|^2$
- Manhattan distance: $|\mathbf{x}_i - \boldsymbol{\mu}_\ell|$

In its simplest form, the procedure consists of the following steps:

1. Divide the objects into k initial clusters and calculate their centers.
2. Each object is assigned to the cluster with the closest center.
3. Once all objects are grouped, the centers are re-calculated.
4. Repeat the process until there are no further changes to cluster members.

The advantages of this algorithm involve its simplicity and speed, which allow it to be suited for large sets of data. However, one main disadvantage is that the global optimal clustering cannot be guaranteed. Instead, the algorithm only provides a local optimal solution, which depends on the initial clustering of the objects. To address this difficulty, the algorithm is commonly applied multiple times, starting from different starting solutions, to find a better clustering result.

4.3.2 *Applying Cluster Analysis to Credit Risk Assessment*

Cluster analysis techniques are useful tools for credit portfolio management, risk analysis, and customer relationship management. Identifying meaningful and homogeneous groups of customers allows credit institutions not only to analyze and get insights into their credit risk exposure but also to provide customized products and services, tailored to their needs of their clients (e.g., lending to construction companies, businesses wholesale, tourism, etc.).

One of the main advantages of clustering approaches is that they do not require historical data on credit defaults. On the other hand, however, such approaches are descriptive, thus being dependent on expert judgment for the interpretation of the results and the derivation of conclusions of practical usefulness.

Clustering techniques have been extensively explored in the literature as there is a strong interest from banking institutions in strengthening their credit decisions. Also, comparisons of the performance of different algorithms to categorize customers into groups of homogeneous features are explored in detail.

One stream in the relevant literature has explored the use of cluster analysis to determine the distribution of losses in loan portfolios of banking institutions. Another application that has been examined involves the construction and pricing of collateralized debt obligations (CDOs).

The characterization and separation of a bank's customers into different bundled categories seeks to identify strategically important bank customers and highlight their credit characteristics. Client profiles incorporate various aspects of their financial status, as well as other information involving the relationship of a customer with a credit institution, the customer's payment history, his/her usage and satisfaction with the provided services, etc.

Such a client profile synthesis system is used in financial companies that can immediately serve customers, knowing in advance their needs and offering services, based only on the analysis of the ratings of the groups that they form. Even if the customer profile is more business-oriented than analytical, it provides a broad picture

Table 4.11 Average credit balance by gender (in €)

Gender	Average credit balance
Males	4641.94
Females	4828.35
Average	4754.48

of the customer real needs. This is an important piece of information for understanding credit behavior.

Customer segmentation also provides approaches that aim, in addition to better understanding of customer group preferences, to more efficient allocation of bank resources based on the available customer information. The benefit to banks is twofold: first, it allows them to differentiate themselves by providing appropriate and specialized services for the needs of their clients and therefore to gain a competitive advantage. Second, customer clustering helps banks and credit institutions to allocate their capital in a more efficient manner among various retail and corporate banking products and services, and customer/regional segments.

The segmentation of clients into risk groups is a basic methodology that should be adopted by banks to better understand and service their customers in an increasingly competitive environment. Market segmentation is one of the central concepts in banking and customer profitability based on customer segmentation criteria is spreading more and more today in many business sectors.

4.3.3 Data and Variables

The data were obtained from Kaggle[1] and they involve a sample of credit card clients in Taiwan from April to September 2005. The sample consists of 23,364 non-defaulted borrowers and 6636 ones in default (default rate 22.12%). Clients in default have delayed payments over 90 days. Except for information about defaults, the data cover several attributes (about 25 overall) involving demographic information as well as information about the credit and payment history of the clients. For instance, among other, there are data about the amount of credit granted to each client, gender, education level, marital status, age of the borrowers, past loan payments, etc.

In total, the sample portfolio involves 142.63 million euros remaining in debt to 30,000 borrowers. The outstanding balances in default (due over 90 days) are 24.51 million euros.

Table 4.11 presents the average balance of credit card debt for the sample portfolio, which for men amounts to 4.6 thousand euros, while for women it is 4.8 thousand euros.

[1]Kaggle is platform for machine learning and data science, with a focus on practical applications. The data used in this study are available at: https://www.kaggle.com/uciml/default-of-credit-card-clients-dataset

Table 4.12 Average credit balance by education level

Education level	Average balance (€)	Number of clients
Graduate school	6045.31	10,585
University	4174.75	14,030
High school	3592.46	4917
Others	6270.66	123
Unknown	4773.78	345

Table 4.13 Average credit balance per marital status

Marital status	Average balance (€)	Number of clients
Married	5172.25	13,659
Single	4440.21	15,964
Other	2784.27	377

Table 4.14 Average credit balance by age

Age range	Average balance (€)	Number of clients
<29	3525.99	9618
30–39	5592.39	11,238
30–40	3745.47	67
40–49	5132.08	6464
50–59	4652.97	2341
≥60	5723.44	272

Table 4.15 Average credit balance (in €) by default status, education level, and gender

		Gender	
Default status	Education level	Males	Females
No default	Graduate school	6494.49	6135.08
	University	4112.05	4695.57
	High school	3765.83	3928.54
	Others	5841.87	6674.73
	Unknown	4666.15	4938.88
	Average	4982.32	5102.00
Default	Graduate school	5194.68	4951.50
	University	2925.46	3394.55
	High school	2551.64	2964.70
	Others	3264.57	5204.39
	Unknown	3860.71	3477.48
	Average	3573.87	3784.84

Table 4.12 presents the average balances of the examined credit card portfolio according to the level of borrower's education. It is evident that most borrowers in this data set (more than 80%) have at least university level education. Table 4.13 provides similar information in terms of the marital status of the borrowers.

Finally, the average lending balance by age is shown in Table 4.14, whereas Table 4.15 provides results for the cross-tabulation by default status, gender, and education level.

Table 4.16 List of variables

Variables code	Interpretation
LIMIT_BAL	Current balance of credit card
GENDER	Male, female
EDU_LEVEL	Education level (postgraduate degree, university-level degree, high school, others, unknown)
MARITAL_STATUS	Married, single, divorced, other
AGE	Age of the borrower in years
AVG_BILL	Average bill statement over the past 6 months (in €)
BILL_DIFF	(Latest -average bill statement)/Range of bill statements over the past 6 months
PAY_BILL	Average (Bill statement – Payment amount)/Current balance
BILL_BAL	Average bill statement/Current balance
N_DEFAULT	Number of defaults in the past 6 months
AVG_BILL_DEF	Average bill amounts in default
MONTHS_DEF	Number of months since last default

The variables available for this data set capture a multitude of customer credit card information and include payment default data. In particular, we have the variables shown in Table 4.16, which take into account particular customer profiles, identifying possible relationships that may exist between different age groups of borrowers, or even between different levels of education.

4.3.4 Results

For this case application, the *k*-medoids algorithm was applied to cluster the sample data into three groups. This is a variant of the *k*-means algorithm, which is suitable for data that include categorical variables, as in the case of this data set. For categorical variables the cluster mean (centroid) is not meaningful. In such cases, clusters can be described by medoids, which are characteristic instances from the data that are representative of the cases belonging in each of the clusters. Thus, medoids are members of the data, in contrast to traditional cluster centroids which are defined by the averages of the cases belonging in the clusters (i.e., they are not existing members of the data).

Before applying a clustering algorithm, the data are commonly scaled to reduce the effect of scale differences among variables. In this case application, all numerical were scaled by their standard deviation. For gender, a dummy variable was introduced taking the value of 1 for males and 0 for females. A similar approach was employed for the marital status, by the introduction of three dummy variables, one indicating married borrowers, one for singles, and another one for divorced clients.

A critical issue in applying partitioning cluster analysis is the definition of the number of clusters. This can be done by examining various cluster performance

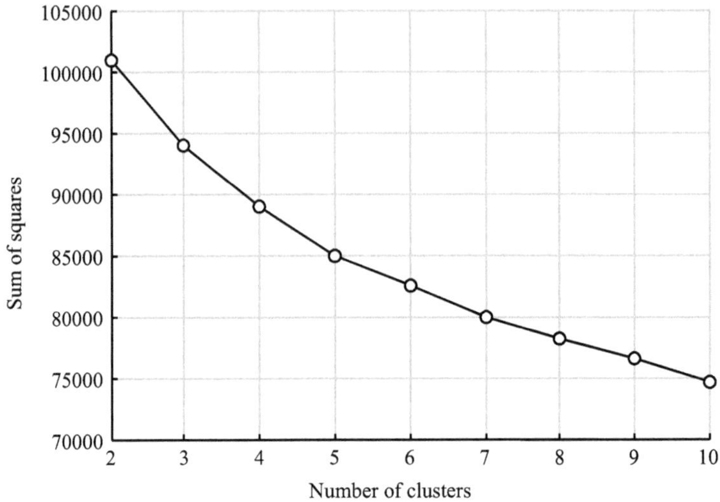

Fig. 4.2 Sum of squared differences from cluster medoids for different number of clusters

Table 4.17 Cluster medoids

Attributes	Cluster 1	Cluster 2	Cluster 3	Cluster 4	Cluster 5
LIMIT_BAL	1987.13	2840	5961.40	6245.27	3122.64
GENDER	Female	Male	Male	Male	Female
MARITAL_STATUS	Single	Married	Married	Single	Single
EDU_LEVEL	University	University	University	Postgraduate	University
AGE	26	41	41	32	31
AVG_BILL	1332.80	1933.54	412.66	550.78	1574.34
BILL_DIFF	−0.10	0.10	−0.03	0.08	0.23
PAY_BILL	0.65	0.74	0.01	0.02	0.54
BILL_BAL	0.67	0.68	0.07	0.09	0.50
N_DEFAULT	4	1	0	0	0
AVG_BILL_DEF	1334.99	37.13	0	0	0
MONTHS_DEF	1	6	No default	No default	No default
Number of members	3982	5532	7646	6847	5993

criteria in relation to the number of clusters. For the purposes of this analysis the sum of squared differences from the cluster medoids is used as the performance metric. The results illustrated in Fig. 4.2 indicate that setting the number of clusters to five is a reasonable choice, providing a reduction in the sum of squared differences of almost 16% compared to the simple two-cluster setting, whereas further increasing the number of clusters to 10 only yields an additional reduction of 12%.

The medoids of the five clusters are presented in Table 4.17. Clusters 1 and 2 can be described as high-risk groups. Cluster 1 consists of 3982 borrowers, whereas cluster 2 includes 5532 cases. The most typical borrowers in these groups (i.e., the

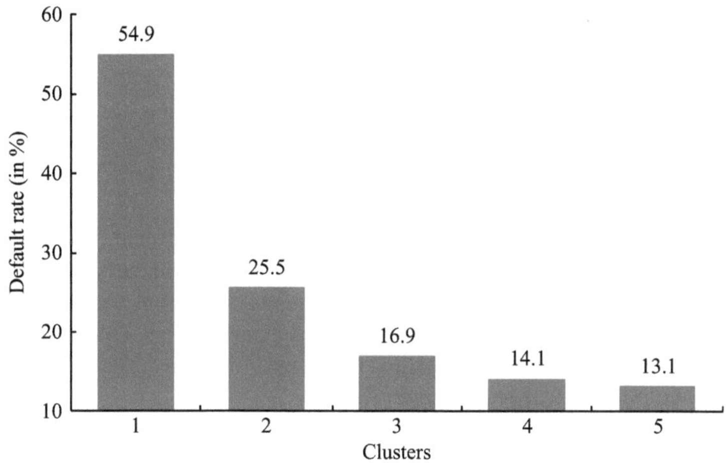

Fig. 4.3 Default rates by cluster

medoids) have defaulted at least once in the past 6 months and their average bill statements is large compared with the payed amounts (PAY_BILL). The same applies to their average bill balance compared to the current balance (BILL_BAL). The rest of the clusters (i.e., clusters 3–5) involve borrowers with no defaults in the past 6 months and lower bill statements compared to their current balances. In terms of the demographic variables, no striking observations can be made. However, it is worth noting that all five typical cluster cases involve borrowers with at least a university-level degree.

Further details about the risk levels of the clusters are provided in Fig. 4.3, which illustrates the default rates for each of the five clusters, i.e., the number of borrowers in a cluster that defaulted over the subsequent period as a ratio of the total number of borrowers in the cluster. This is an external validation of the clusters relying on the known default status of the borrowers. The results confirm the descriptive observations made earlier regarding the characteristics of the typical borrowers describing the clusters. Indeed, the default rate is almost 55% for cluster 1 and more than 25% for cluster 2, whereas clusters 3–5 have much lower default rates, ranging between 13.1% and 16.9%.

4.3.5 Perspectives

Descriptive methodologies, such as unsupervised data analysis techniques complement predictive models developed with supervised machine learning and operations research techniques, providing useful insights about the properties of the data before predictive models can be developed. Moreover, they facilitate the identification of hidden patterns in the data and the formulation of data segments with homogeneous characteristics. Data segmentation is often important for decision making and predictive modeling, as analytical models work best when calibrated for meaningful and homogeneous parts of data.

Cluster analysis algorithms, either hierarchical or partitioning, can be very helpful in this context, as tools for analytical descriptive analysis in a multidimensional context, or for data pre-processing prior to predictive and prescriptive decision support.

In the illustrative application presented above, a partitional cluster analysis algorithm, namely the k-medoids algorithm was used to identify homogeneous groups borrowers in a credit risk assessment context from retail banking, based on the characteristics and past credit behavior of credit card holders. External validation against the actual status of the borrowers showed that the derived clusters are associated with different levels of credit risk.

4.4 Notes and References

The use of analytical models for credit scoring and rating has gained much interest in the academic literature over the past couple of decades. While early research, mainly focused in corporate financial distress prediction models (Sun et al. 2014), credit risk analysis also became popular due to the establishment of new regulatory standards in the financial sector and the increasing availability of relevant data.

Nowadays, there is a vast literature in this area with numerous applications and empirical results for various countries and different contexts (e.g., corporate loans and consumer credit). Among others, one can mention applications in:

- Microfinance and SMEs (Altman and Sabato 2007; Angilella and Mazzù 2015; Li et al. 2016; Oliveira et al. 2017; Sohn and Kim 2013; Van Gool et al. 2012).
- Bond ratings (Kao and Lee 2012; Livingston et al. 2018; Mizen and Tsoukas 2012).
- Sector studies (Sohn and Kim 2013; Szczerba and Ciemski 2009; Van Gestel et al. 2007; Voulgaris and Lemonakis 2014).
- Country-specific and cross-country studies (Akkoç 2012; Dinh and Kleimeier 2007; Doumpos et al. 2015; Lemonakis et al. 2015; Nguyen 2015; Nikolic et al. 2013).
- Behavioral and profit scoring (Adams et al. 2001; Bravo et al. 2015; Chamboko and Bravo 2016; Crook et al. 2007; Sanchez-Barrios et al. 2016; Sarlija et al. 2009; Serrano-Cinca and Gutiérrez-Nieto 2016).
- Methodological advances (Akkoç 2012; Alves and Dias 2015; Bijak and Thomas 2012; HSIEH 2005; Jones et al. 2015; Kvamme et al. 2018; Luo et al. 2009).
- New financing platforms (Emekter et al. 2015; Garefalakis et al. 2017; Jiang et al. 2018; Serrano-Cinca and Gutiérrez-Nieto 2016; Vanneschi et al. 2018).

Chapter 5
Conclusions and Future Research

Credit risk measurement and management is an active area of research that combines elements from various disciplines. As new forms of credit gain ground (e.g., from traditional corporate and consumer loans to crowdfunding, social lending, etc.) and tighter regulatory requirements are imposed (Basel accords and new reporting and accounting standards such as IFRS 9), new opportunities and challenges arise for practitioners and researchers.

While analytical models are not new in this area (they have been used at least since the 1970–1980s), they are now more relevant than ever before, as they enable the rapid processing of massive amounts of data, the discovery of complex relationships between many interconnecting factors, the analysis of various scenarios, and the identification of patterns that characterize the behavior and decisions taken by both borrowers and lenders.

The practice of credit risk assessment has traditionally been dominated by statistical techniques and financial models, including methods like discriminant analysis, logit/probit analysis, hazard models, as well as market-based approaches inspired by the works of Black, Scholes, and Merton. However, alternative approaches have been gaining ground recently, partly due to massive datasets becoming more relevant, with information derived from various sources, beyond the ones traditional used in financial models (e.g., financial and market-based data). For instance, information from social media and other online sources and corporate networks, provide a plethora of new information that has the potential to enhance credit risk analysis leading to a new era of risk measurement systems that will provide more comprehensive insights and predictions on loan performance and defaults. Thus, data-driven approaches that enable the analysis of such enriched data sets are of great importance. Operations research and management science techniques have the potential to contribute in this new framework, providing different tools for model building and assessment, including optimization models, metaheuristics, stochastic models, decision analysis, as well as network techniques.

M. Doumpos et al., *Analytical Techniques in the Assessment of Credit Risk*, EURO Advanced Tutorials on Operational Research,
https://doi.org/10.1007/978-3-319-99411-6_5

However, despite the progress achieved so far, there are still many open issues worth of further consideration. For instance, an important aspect that one must bear in mind when introducing more sophisticated models is comprehensibility and transparency. Improved and more powerful models introduced in academic research are often not adopted in practice, because they are not comprehensible and transparent for the end users. A model or system that lacks these qualities operates like a black-box, which raises concerns on whether its recommendations can be justified and interpreted to top management, auditors, as well as supervisors and other external authorities. Moreover, black-box approaches are much more difficult to calibrate and customize to the changing needs of financial institutions and other users of credit risk assessment systems. Domain expertise from expert credit analysts and data analysts is also difficult to incorporate into systems that are incomprehensible. This may raise concerns on the performance of the models in the long-run. Finally, one also needs to consider the organizational burden that would be needed to adopt and incorporate complex systems into the daily operations of the end-user organization. This burden is generally higher for complex credit risk assessment models, as they may require extra costs for development, calibration, maintenance, special software requirements, personnel training, etc. Thus, maintaining a balanced tradeoff between model performance and comprehensibility is an important issue for further consideration.

Assessing the performance of credit risk assessment systems is also an open area of research. Traditionally, statistical performance criteria are employed to evaluate the predictive power of credit models. Such performance metrics constitute a common basis, which is acceptable and well-understood by researchers, credit risk modelers, and supervisors. However, financial performance attributes should also be considered. The connections between statistical predictive power and financial performance attributes has attracted some interest in the relevant literature. However, further analysis is needed in this area. The main difficulty towards this direction is that financial criteria require case-specific information (e.g., costs for accepting bad credits or rejecting good ones), which are usually subjective and change over time.

On the methodological side, further emphasis could be put on scaling up existing modeling techniques to big data. This is particularly important, given the recent trends on the use of massive data sets for credit risk analysis as well as in other related financial risk management areas. Big data analytics involve the interplay between traditional operations research/management science techniques, with advances in computer science. This goes beyond standard algorithmic advancements in solution techniques, as issues like data storage and handling, distributed computing and parallel processing, visualization and reporting, become also relevant. This area opens many new possibilities for modeling new types of information and analyzing complex relationships between borrowers and different markets, including deeper analysis of systemic risks and default correlations.

Finally, it is worth noting that the use of analytical modeling techniques for credit risk assessment covers several other areas, beyond credit scoring and rating systems, which have not been addressed in this book. Among many examples, one can mention Markov chain models for the analysis of credit migration, stochastic models for risk management in credit derivatives, optimization approaches for credit portfolio optimization and management, as well as metaheuristics for the calibration of credit scoring scorecards. Combined with the above areas of research, these issues leave a lot of open room for further applications of operations research approaches and other analytical tools in credit risk modeling.

References

Adams, N. M., Hand, D. J., & Till, R. J. (2001). Mining for classes and patterns in behavioural data. *Journal of the Operational Research Society, 52*(9), 1017–1024.

Agarwal, V., & Taffler, R. (2008). Comparing the performance of market-based and accounting-based bankruptcy prediction models. *Journal of Banking and Finance, 32*(8), 1541–1551.

Akkoç, S. (2012). An empirical comparison of conventional techniques, neural networks and the three stage hybrid Adaptive Neuro Fuzzy Inference System (ANFIS) model for credit scoring analysis: The case of Turkish credit card data. *European Journal of Operational Research, 222* (1), 168–178.

Almeida, H., Cunha, I., Ferreira, M. A., & Restrepo, F. (2017). The real effects of credit ratings: The sovereign ceiling channel. *The Journal of Finance, 72*(1), 249–290.

Altman, E. I. (1968). Financial ratios, discriminant analysis and the prediction of corporate bankruptcy. *The Journal of Finance, 23*(4), 589–609.

Altman, E. I., & Sabato, G. (2007). Modelling credit risk for SMEs: Evidence from the U.S. market. *Abacus, 43*(3), 332–357.

Altman, E. I., & Saunders, A. (1997). Credit risk measurement: Developments over the last 20 years. *Journal of Banking and Finance, 21*(11–12), 1721–1742.

Altman, E. I., Haldeman, R. G., & Narayanan, P. (1977). ZETA™ analysis – A new model to identify bankruptcy risk of corporations. *Journal of Banking and Finance, 1*(1), 29–54.

Alves, B. C., & Dias, J. G. (2015). Survival mixture models in behavioral scoring. *Expert Systems with Applications, 42*(8), 3902–3910.

Angilella, S., & Mazzù, S. (2015). The financing of innovative SMEs: A multicriteria credit rating model. *European Journal of Operational Research, 244*(2), 540–554.

Anson, M. J. P., Fabozzi, F. J., Chen, R-R., & Choudhry, M. (2008). Credit risk modeling using reduced-form models. In F. J. Fabozzi (Ed.), *Handbook of finance* (Vol. III, pp. 277–286). Hoboken, NJ: Wiley.

Baesens, B., Setiono, R., Mues, C., & Vanthienen, J. (2003). Using neural network rule extraction and decision tables for credit-risk evaluation. *Management Science, 49*(3), 312–329.

Basel Committee on Banking Supervision. (2005). *Studies on the validation of internal rating systems*. Switzerland: Basel.

Berger, A. N., Frame, W. S., & Miller, N. H. (2005). Credit scoring and the availability, price, and risk of small business credit. *Journal of Money, Credit and Banking, 37*(2), 191–222.

Berger, A. N., Cowan, A. M., & Frame, W. S. (2011). The surprising use of credit scoring in small business lending by community banks and the attendant effects on credit availability, risk, and profitability. *Journal of Financial Services Research, 39*(1–2), 1–17.

M. Doumpos et al., *Analytical Techniques in the Assessment of Credit Risk*, EURO Advanced Tutorials on Operational Research,
https://doi.org/10.1007/978-3-319-99411-6

Bharath, S. T., & Shumway, T. (2008). Forecasting default with the Merton distance to default model. *Review of Financial Studies, 21*(3), 1339–1369.
Bijak, K., & Thomas, L. C. (2012). Does segmentation always improve model performance in credit scoring? *Expert Systems with Applications, 39*(3), 2433–2442.
Black, F., & Scholes, M. (1973). The pricing of options and corporate liabilities. *Journal of Political Economy, 81*(3), 637–659.
Blöchlinger, A., & Leippold, M. (2006). Economic benefit of powerful credit scoring. *Journal of Banking and Finance, 30*(3), 851–873.
Bolton, P., Freixas, X., & Shapiro, J. (2012). The credit ratings game. *The Journal of Finance, 67*(1), 85–111.
Bravo, C., Thomas, L. C., & Weber, R. (2015). Improving credit scoring by differentiating defaulter behaviour. *Journal of the Operational Research Society, 66*(5), 771–781.
Bugera, V., Konno, H., & Uryasev, S. (2002). Credit cards scoring with quadratic utility functions. *Journal of Multi-Criteria Decision Analysis, 11*(4–5), 197–211.
Campbell, J. Y., Hilscher, J., & Szilagyi, J. (2008). In search of distress risk. *The Journal of Finance, 63*(6), 2899–2939.
Chamboko, R., & Bravo, J. M. (2016). On the modelling of prognosis from delinquency to normal performance on retail consumer loans. *Risk Management, 18*(4), 264–287.
Chava, S., & Jarrow, R. A. (2004). Bankruptcy prediction with industry effects. *Review of Finance, 8*(4), 537–569.
Chen, J., & Hill, P. (2013). The impact of diverse measures of default risk on UK stock returns. *Journal of Banking and Finance, 37*, 5118.
Crook, J. N., Edelman, D. B., & Thomas, L. C. (2007). Recent developments in consumer credit risk assessment. *European Journal of Operational Research, 183*(3), 1447–1465.
Crosbie, P., & Bohn, J. (2003). *Modeling default risk*. New York: Moody's KMV.
Desai, V. S., Crook, J. N., & Overstreet, G. A. (1996). A comparison of neural networks and linear scoring models in the credit union environment. *European Journal of Operational Research, 95*(1), 24–37.
Dimitras, A. I., Zanakis, S. H., & Zopounidis, C. (1996). A survey of business failures with an emphasis on prediction methods and industrial applications. *European Journal of Operational Research, 90*(3), 487–513.
Dinh, T. H. T., & Kleimeier, S. (2007). A credit scoring model for Vietnam's retail banking market. *International Review of Financial Analysis, 16*(5), 471–495.
Doumpos, M., & Pasiouras, F. (2005). Developing and testing models for replicating credit ratings: A multicriteria approach. *Computational Economics, 25*(4), 327–341.
Doumpos, M., & Zopounidis, C. (2011). A multicriteria ouranking modeling approach for credit rating. *Decision Sciences, 42*(3), 721–742.
Doumpos, M., Kosmidou, K., Baourakis, G., & Zopounidis, C. (2002). Credit risk assessment using a multicriteria hierarchical discrimination approach: A comparative analysis. *European Journal of Operational Research, 138*(2), 392–412.
Doumpos, M., Niklis, D., Zopounidis, C., & Andriosopoulos, K. (2015). Combining accounting data and a structural model for predicting credit ratings: Empirical evidence from European listed firms. *Journal of Banking and Finance, 50*, 599–607.
Duffie, D., & Singleton, K. J. (1999). Modeling term structures of defaultable bonds. *Review of Financial Studies, 12*(4), 687–720.
Einav, L., Jenkins, M., & Levin, J. (2013). The impact of credit scoring on consumer lending. *The RAND Journal of Economics, 44*(2), 249–274.
Emekter, R., Tu, Y., Jirasakuldech, B., & Lu, M. (2015). Evaluating credit risk and loan performance in online peer-to-peer (P2P) lending. *Applied Economics, 47*(1), 54–70.
Forcella, D. (2015). *European microfinance credit risk management and credit scoring – State of the art and perspective*. Brussels: European Microfinance Network.
Frame, W. S., Srinivasan, A., & Woosley, L. (2001). The effect of credit scoring on small-business lending. *Journal of Money, Credit and Banking, 33*(3), 813–825.

Frost, C. A. (2007). Credit rating agencies in capital markets: A review of research evidence on selected criticisms of the agencies. *Journal of Accounting, Auditing and Finance, 22*(3), 469–492.

Frydman, H., Altman, E. I., & Kao, D.-L. (1985). Introducing recursive partitioning for financial classification: The case of financial distress. *The Journal of Finance, 40*(1), 269.

Galindo, J., & Tamayo, P. (2000). Credit risk assessment using statistical and machine learning: Basic methodology and risk modeling applications. *Computational Economics, 15*(1/2), 107–143.

Garefalakis, A., Alexopoulos, G., Tsatsaronis, M., & Lemonakis, C. (2017). Financial and investment strategies to captivate S&P 500 volatility premium. *Investment Management and Financial Innovations, 14*(3), 39–53.

Hillegeist, S. A., Keating, E. K., Cram, D. P., & Lundstedt, K. G. (2004). Assessing the probability of bankruptcy. *Review of Accounting Studies, 9*(1), 5–34.

Hilscher, J., & Wilson, M. (2017). Credit ratings and credit risk: Is one measure enough? *Management Science, 63*(10), 3414–3437.

Hsieh, N. (2005). Hybrid mining approach in the design of credit scoring models. *Expert Systems with Applications, 28*(4), 655–665.

Jarrow, R., & Turnbull, S. M. (1992). Credit risk: Drawing the analogy. *Risk Magazine, 5*(9), 63–70.

Jarrow, R. A., & Turnbull, S. M. (1995). Pricing derivatives on financial securities subject to credit risk. *The Journal of Finance, 50*(1), 53–85.

Jeon, D.-S., & Lovo, S. (2013). Credit rating industry: A helicopter tour of stylized facts and recent theories. *International Journal of Industrial Organization, 31*(5), 643–651.

Jiang, C., Wang, Z., Wang, R., & Ding, Y. (2018). Loan default prediction by combining soft information extracted from descriptive text in online peer-to-peer lending. *Annals of Operations Research, 266*(1–2), 511–529.

Jones, S., Johnstone, D., & Wilson, R. (2015). An empirical evaluation of the performance of binary classifiers in the prediction of credit ratings changes. *Journal of Banking and Finance, 56*, 72–85.

Kao, L.-J., & Lee, C.-F. (2012). Alternative method for determining industrial bond ratings: Theory and empirical evidence. *International Journal of Information Technology and Decision Making, 11*(6), 1215–1235.

Kisgen, D. J. (2006). Credit ratings and capital structure. *The Journal of Finance, 61*(3), 1035–1072.

Kisgen, D. J. (2009). Do firms target credit ratings or leverage levels? *Journal of Financial and Quantitative Analysis, 44*(6), 1323–1344.

Kvamme, H., Sellereite, N., Aas, K., & Sjursen, S. (2018). Predicting mortgage default using convolutional neural networks. *Expert Systems with Applications, 102*, 207–217.

Lemonakis, C., Voulgaris, F., Vassakis, K., & Christakis, S. (2015). Efficiency, capital and risk in banking industry: The case of Middle East and North Africa (MENA) countries. *International Journal of Financial Engineering and Risk Management, 2*(2), 109.

Lemonakis, C., Garefalakis, A., Giannarakis, G., Tabouratzi, E., & Zopounidis, C. (2017). Innovation and SMEs financial distress during the crisis period: The Greek paradigm. In C. Floros & I. Chatziantoniou (Eds.), *The Greek debt crisis* (pp. 285–308). Cham: Palgrave Macmillan.

Lessmann, S., Baesens, B., Seow, H.-V., & Thomas, L. C. (2015). Benchmarking state-of-the-art classification algorithms for credit scoring: An update of research. *European Journal of Operational Research, 247*(1), 124–136.

Li, K., Niskanen, J., Kolehmainen, M., & Niskanen, M. (2016). Financial innovation: Credit default hybrid model for SME lending. *Expert Systems with Applications, 61*, 343–355.

Livingston, M., Poon, W. P. H., & Zhou, L. (2018). Are Chinese credit ratings relevant? A study of the Chinese bond market and credit rating industry. *Journal of Banking and Finance, 87*, 216–232.

Luo, S.-T., Cheng, B.-W., & Hsieh, C.-H. (2009). Prediction model building with clustering-launched classification and support vector machines in credit scoring. *Expert Systems with Applications, 36*(4), 7562–7566.

Martens, D., Baesens, B., Van Gestel, T., & Vanthienen, J. (2007). Comprehensible credit scoring models using rule extraction from support vector machines. *European Journal of Operational Research, 183*(3), 1466–1476.

Merton, R. C. (1974). On the pricing of corporate debt: The risk structure of interest rates. *The Journal of Finance, 29*(2), 449–470.

Mester, L. J. (1997). What's the point of credit scoring? *Business Review*, (September/October), 3–16.

Mizen, P., & Tsoukas, S. (2012). Forecasting US bond default ratings allowing for previous and initial state dependence in an ordered probit model. *International Journal of Forecasting, 28*(1), 273–287.

Nguyen, H.-T. (2015). Default predictors in credit scoring: Evidence from France's retail banking institution. *The Journal of Credit Risk, 11*(2), 41–66.

Niklis, D., Doumpos, M., & Zopounidis, C. (2014). Combining market and accounting-based models for credit scoring using a classification scheme based on support vector machines. *Applied Mathematics and Computation, 234*, 69–81.

Nikolic, N., Zarkic-Joksimovic, N., Stojanovski, D., & Joksimovic, I. (2013). The application of brute force logistic regression to corporate credit scoring models: Evidence from Serbian financial statements. *Expert Systems with Applications, 40*(15), 5932–5944.

Ohlson, J. A. (1980). Financial ratios and the probabilistic prediction of bankruptcy. *Journal of Accounting Research, 18*(1), 109.

Oliveira, M. D. N. T., Ferreira, F. A. F., Pérez-Bustamante Ilander, G. O., & Jalali, M. S. (2017). Integrating cognitive mapping and MCDA for bankruptcy prediction in small- and medium-sized enterprises. *Journal of the Operational Research Society, 68*(9), 985–997.

Oliver, R. M. (2013). Financial performance measures in credit scoring. *EURO Journal on Decision Processes, 1*(3–4), 169–185.

Papageorgiou, D., Doumpos, M., Zopounidis, C., & Pardalos, P. M. (2008). Credit rating systems: Regulatory framework and comparative evaluation of existing methods. In C. Zopounidis, M. Doumpos, & P. M. Pardalos (Eds.), *Handbook of financial engineering* (pp. 457–488). New York: Springer.

Piramuthu, S. (1999). Financial credit-risk evaluation with neural and neurofuzzy systems. *European Journal of Operational Research, 112*(2), 310–321.

Sanchez-Barrios, L. J., Andreeva, G., & Ansell, J. (2016). Time-to-profit scorecards for revolving credit. *European Journal of Operational Research, 249*(2), 397–406.

Sarlija, N., Bensic, M., & Zekic-Susac, M. (2009). Comparison procedure of predicting the time to default in behavioural scoring. *Expert Systems with Applications, 36*(5), 8778–8788.

Serrano-Cinca, C., & Gutiérrez-Nieto, B. (2016). The use of profit scoring as an alternative to credit scoring systems in peer-to-peer (P2P) lending. *Decision Support Systems, 89*, 113–122.

Sobehart, J. R., Keenan, S. C., & Stein, R. (2000). *Benchmarking quantitative default risk models: A validation methodology*. New York: Moody's Investors Service.

Sohn, S. Y., & Kim, Y. S. (2013). Behavioral credit scoring model for technology-based firms that considers uncertain financial ratios obtained from relationship banking. *Small Business Economics, 41*(4), 931–943.

Srinivasan, V., & Kim, Y. H. (1987). Credit granting: A comparative analysis of classification procedures. *The Journal of Finance, 42*(3), 665–681.

Sun, J., Li, H., Huang, Q.-H., & He, K.-Y. (2014). Predicting financial distress and corporate failure: A review from the state-of-the-art definitions, modeling, sampling, and featuring approaches. *Knowledge-Based Systems, 57*, 41–56.

Szczerba, M., & Ciemski, A. (2009). Credit risk handling in telecommunication sector (pp. 117–130).

Tabouratzi, E., Lemonakis, C., & Garefalakis, A. (2017). Determinants of failure in greek manufacturing SMEs. *Corporate Ownership and Control, 14*(3), 45–50.

Thomas, L. C. (2009). Modelling the credit risk for portfolios of consumer loans: Analogies with corporate loan models. *Mathematics and Computers in Simulation, 79*(8), 2525–2534.

Thomas, L. C., Edelman, D. B., & Crook, J. N. (2002). *Credit scoring and its applications*. Philadelphia: SIAM.

Tichy, G., Lannoo, K., Gwilym, O., Alsakka, R., Masciandaro, D., & Paudyn, B. (2011). Credit rating agencies: Part of the solution or part of the problem? *Intereconomics, 46*(5), 232–262.

van Deventer, D. R., Imai, K., & Mesler, M. (2013). *Reduced form credit models and credit model testing. Advanced financial risk management* (2nd ed.). Singapore: Wiley.

Van Gestel, T., & Baesens, B. (2009). *Credit risk management – Basic concepts*. Oxford: Oxford University Press.

Van Gestel, T., Martens, D., Baesens, B., Feremans, D., Huysmans, J., & Vanthienen, J. (2007). Forecasting and analyzing insurance companies' ratings. *International Journal of Forecasting, 23*(3), 513–529.

Van Gool, J., Verbeke, W., Sercu, P., & Baesens, B. (2012). Credit scoring for microfinance: Is it worth it? *International Journal of Finance and Economics, 17*(2), 103–123.

Vanneschi, L., Horn, D. M., Castelli, M., & Popovič, A. (2018). An artificial intelligence system for predicting customer default in e-commerce. *Expert Systems with Applications, 104*, 1–21.

Voulgaris, F., & Lemonakis, C. (2014). Competitiveness and profitability: The case of chemicals, pharmaceuticals and plastics. *The Journal of Economic Asymmetries, 11*, 46–57.

West, D. (2000). Neural network credit scoring models. *Computers and Operations Research, 27* (11–12), 1131–1152.

Zavgren, C. V. (1985). Assessing the vulnerability to failure of American industrial firms: A logistic analysis. *Journal of Business Finance and Accounting, 12*(1), 19–45.

Zhang, Z., Gao, G., & Shi, Y. (2014). Credit risk evaluation using multi-criteria optimization classifier with kernel, fuzzification and penalty factors. *European Journal of Operational Research, 237*(1), 335–348.

Index

M. Doumpos et al., *Analytical Techniques in the Assessment of Credit Risk*, EURO Advanced Tutorials on Operational Research,
https://doi.org/10.1007/978-3-319-99411-6

MIX
Papier aus verantwortungsvollen Quellen
Paper from responsible sources
FSC® C105338

If you have any concerns about our products,
you can contact us on
ProductSafety@springernature.com

In case Publisher is established outside the EU,
the EU authorized representative is:
Springer Nature Customer Service Center GmbH
Europaplatz 3, 69115 Heidelberg, Germany

Printed by Libri Plureos GmbH
in Hamburg, Germany